Jay R. Midas Chapters [Transcribed]: Ch. 1.0 - 4.0

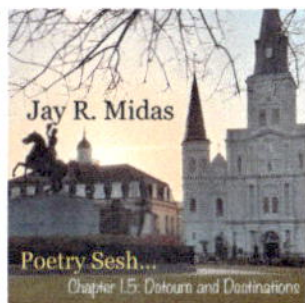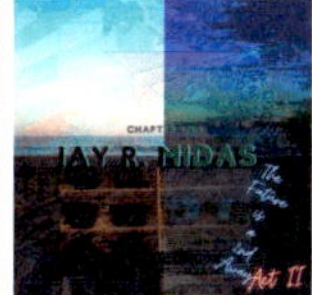

jayrmidas.com

Chapter 1.0 *The Beginning is Present*

Chapter 1.5 *Detours and Destinations*

Chapter 2.0 *The Past is EterNaL*

Chapter 2.5* *future!TENSE.*

Chapter 3.0 *The Future is a 2nd Away*

Chapter 3.0.1 *The Future is a 2nd Away Act II*

Chapter 3.0.2 TFi2A Act II: *The NeedeRealm Trials*

Chapter 3.5 TFi2A Act II: *Dissent into 2088*

Chapter 4.0 *Convergence 2088*

YouTube

Spotify

Jay R. Midas- Cover Letter & Bio

Image by Jamal Morris @a.lucid.dreamer (Instagram)

Jay R. Midas is a Nuyorican Poet and Coach who has roots in two boroughs Brooklyn and Queens, NY. Born in St. John's Queens *(defunct)* hospital, raised in Marcy Houses, Midas always had a creative nature and a calling for leadership. His work covers a myriad of topics such as love, philosophy, self-discovery and societal quandaries. Writing poetry since youth, Jay found he best expressed himself on paper when speaking up and speaking out was a challenge. As an adolescent, Midas created opportunities to connect people in a meaningful way. During his college years Midas changed direction to incorporate rhythm when he and two close friends recorded music as Lyrics Flow Delivery. For Midas, a second generation American overcoming hurdles and generational obstacles, this form of expression is considered a right of passage. He and several others would go on to create ***Real Artist Group Entertainment***, a pact which united a group of artists and friends to collaborate and set events- "Battle at the Beach", recording sessions and collaborations with independent network, Robb Entertainment are a few examples.

Midas moved to Queens, NY where he would find a home in peaceful Forest Hills developing as an adult and as a professional for over a decade before finding belonging in storied Ridgewood, where Brooklyn and Queens kiss. A career in Athletics and Physical Education, a couple of Podcasts later (***3RG Podcast*** and ***Open the Box)*** respectively, Jay Rando Midas would change course once again where in late 2021 when he developed the Spotify channel, ***Jay R. Midas Chapters***. What started off as an aural experience with an originally created soundbyte poem outro, became a full-on RPG-like adventure chronicle spanning over 5 full chapters with twists, winding loops and Jay R. Midas having to confront his most ferocious opponent… himself. You may now find Chapters on Amazon, Kindle, Spotify, YouTube, Apple Podcasts, Zencastr and coming to Audible. Jay R. Midas currently provides mentorship for people of all ages and spends time performing in the poetry and arts community- hosting local events, performing at local mics such as Nuyorican Slam Competitions, Sissy McGinty's hosted by Jason Hazell, Afro Bros Open Mic at the Witching Hour, and the Stoner Circus Concert Series hosted by Negus and Capital Q & amazing camera work done by @irrregular_shots (Instagram). Jay loves to share meaningful conversations with others, helping strengthen self-esteem and confidence in the modern world. Currently, Midas organizes events within his community of Ridgewood, NY. Jay's favorite location is Aftermath NYC, home of Poetry Shuffle and Sugarplum Humbug. Of course, shout out to the recently departed Craft Culture (RIP)- Thanks for the memories Caesar, Rody & CJ!

Jay R. Midas Chapters [Transcribed]: Ch. 1.0 - 1.5

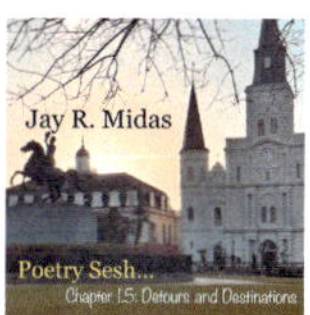

jayrmidas.com

Chapter 1.0 *The Beginning is Present*

Chapter 1.5 *Detours and Destinations*

Chapter 2.0 *The Past is EterNaL*

Chapter III *future!TENSE.*

Chapter 3.0 *The Future is a 2nd Away*

Chapter 3.0.1 *The Future is a 2nd Away Act II*

Chapter 3.0.2 TFi2A Act II: *The NeedeRealm Trials*

Chapter 3.5 TFi2A Act II: *Dissent into 2088*

Chapter 4.0 *Convergence 2088*

Chapter 1.0 *The Beginning is Present*

"Long Term"
"Behind the Wins"
"Liberty is My Name"
"Mr. Almost"
"Turning the Heavy Wheel Back to Unity"

"Long Term"

I saw our future the other day.
At least, the one I hope we live out.
In the latter stages of our lives,
When we had been through the struggle, the milestones,
The house, the children who have long moved out.
There is us. Sitting, dining, laughing without worry of responsibility,
Time or ambition which distracts us from each other.

May I be forever blessed with your love, eternally enamored by your beauty and endlessly charmed by your wit.
You are capable of achieving anything in this world.
And I look forward to the day where you achieve everything you want out of it.
May we adapt to every change, carry each other through every hurdle
And forgive each other when we inevitably falter.

You are my hero, partner and best friend.
And forces will try to drive a wedge between us.
But you have seen what I have done for others I didn't feel half for.
Imagine what I am willing to do for you.

"Behind the uuins"

"Behind the Wins"

You only see the wins.
The small victories.
The things you say that make me special.
But what you don't see are the losses I take…everyday.
L after L after L, big or small.
I take it all to the chin
Because I know…
Victory is on the horizon.
My spirit is timelessly tested.
My soul is perpetually protected.
My body continues to prop me up and keep me going another day.
Speak less.
Listen more.
Speak up!
Don't listen to the noise.
Listen to the voice that is deep inside… you.
The voice of my mom who demands I confront obstacles as she did.
The voice of my dad who has an unwavering belief in me, as I share in him.
The therapeutic laughter and joy of my younger sister.
The silent courage of my baby brother.
The advice of my day ones.
And a whole other litany of people to make proud.
The pressure is on.
But whatever I do, I better wake up ready to win.
Every day.

"LiBerTy is mY nAmE"

Is the world evil or good?
I'm undecided.
As we stand on the hills of borrowed philosophies, a species divided,
We have lost care for the natural, bountiful and ever replenishing,
Earth.
And now we seek to wreak havoc
on our Solar System?
We claim things by calling dibs or throwing a conceptualized currency which buys motivation.
Motivation which is then stifled by hustle.
Hustle in turn distracts us from fulfillment.
Fulfillment in our truest purpose…
To live for the self,
And for the world around you.
Only then can we truly make the world,
A better place.
But why does my happiness have to come at the cost of someone's despair?
That doesn't seem fair.
In order to achieve peace, we have a lot to unlearn.
It is easier create division, start wars,
And inflict violence.
Quite frankly, I'm tired of easy.
If you are feeling courageous,
Stand by me.
Let's forge a new path,
And set a course toward being free.

"Mr. Almost"

I am here to kill Mr. Almost.
Missed opportunities and prioritizing things that just don't matter.
You lose things.
Forget.
Disagree with yourself.
And debate the air.
Where's the fanfare?
The selfcare?
The hardware?
The extra layer?
Saving yourself from an existence of despair because you know the right people are,
Aware.
But they will not recognize Mr. Almost.
You build people up for a return equivalent to imaginary numbers.
You have allowed empires to fall on your watch.
But the true travesty is that you don't walk around like you should.
Worth your weight in precious metals.
Mr. Almost walked away from fights he knew he could win.
He got entangled with those who would inevitably help him to lose.
And always gave the power to his opposition.
But you have become a great from the reactive side of the chessboard.
From pillow fights to the war of words, Mr. Almost had nothing in his mind's eye.
No tomorrow lined up.
Yesterday never existed.
The future is another day.
Mr. Almost, the world needs you to save it now.
Can you do that?

...Say goodbye to Mr. Almost.

"Steering the Heavy Wheel Toward Unity"

Disregard human rights violations, all for the sake of vaccination.

Welcome home to Vaccine Nation.

People fought hard for a choice, now left without a voice, so when they speak, it's simply noise.

It is their right to be wrong, but it's also wrong to push our rights upon someone who wishes to carry along, thinking the way they do…

and now because we are afraid of the cold and flu, people can now take advantage of you.

Privilege has been separated by race, by color, by beliefs, by faith and now by the brand of shots it takes.

To keep you healthy?

Or at least less sick?

Help me.

Because I can't understand how Big Business stood wealthy, reporting **their** losses, OUR loss of life.

To the tune of the Pied Piper's media fife. We drowned in the oceans because we chose to take sides.

All to this plan we carried along, to the sound of sirens sounding off that wretched song. And soon we'll see that we all were wrong.

But all things considered, we handled it well.

At least when we cough, we don't end up in a cell, and score one for science who kept us from hell.

There is only one true answer you see.

The true choice is unity.

Because the true disease is inhumanity.

Thank you.

Chapter 1.5 *Detours and Destinations*
"D-Side Interlude"
"Chills n' Hot Flashes"
"Nola."
"Nu-Your-E-Kin"
"Moving Day"

Life flips upside down from Chapter 1.0 The Beginning is Present. A lot of change has happened in a brief period. Many questions are still hanging in the balance. A life changing trip to New Orleans set the *directions* for the story that unfolds today. Holding an audio recorder, heading to a conference, a mild mannered PE teacher became rushed with poet energy, and while trying to find his way to the conference center whilst simultaneously working on finding his way through life, he would freestyle some important questions. "D-Side" Interlude aptly encapsulates the essence of Chapter 1.5- Detours and Destinations. Chapter 1.5 Ep. 2 would later become works like Chapter 3.0 Ep. 3 "Who Will You Become?" ,

A call to your inner spirit to actively question your purpose and perspective.

"D-Side Interlude"

"Do I need to be on this side or this, or this side? I can barely D-Side. Because I think, right now I got to D-Side myself from picking A-Side. That make sense? And you flip it over to the B-Side and you C, that the grass isn't always greener as you would like it to B. But you need to C what side you truly are on. But as I said, I have to D-Side. What side do I take? Because even if I go left, I'm right."

"Chills n' Hot Flashes"

Cold.

That's how it feels without you. The blankets we shared cannot replace the warmth of your arms around me.

Warm,

My heart has to be because I now know that I am not an individual, I am a Movement. A Movement does not have time to stop. But I will always stop for you. Yet, I pick up my feet to catch up to your pace.

Hot!

You. Me. Vacationing somewhere tropical. Love, trust and understanding. A deep personal bond. Belief in each other, belief in ourselves.

Also Hot…

Hot Headed I could be sometimes. Hard on myself. Unfocused. Fighting through feelings. Worrying before I faced things heads on. You took that on with me, thank you for it all.

I wish it was you.

I hope it is you.

But, if not.

Know that you still have my…

Time…
Love…
and Respect.

And as my role changes in your life- near or far, I am here for you if you need me.

Okay, cool.

"Nola."

I love you, Nola.
You eat stress for breakfast…and still have a high quality of life.
No matter what the day brings.
One can still see hope in your eyes.
Affectionate, kind and real.
Real sexy.
And you know it.
Even in the midst of your most gritty sides…
You still emanate beauty.
You are a teacher of life lessons,
Both historical and contemporary
You are the line of responsibility and freedom.
Your spirit in my glass and in my soul,
Fills me up inside.
You're everything that my current commitment wants to be.
But her heart is not in it anymore.
Responsibility without love is simply Ny [nigh], N-Y.
Nola,
I passed away in your arms and
Was reborn within your legs.
And if I'm being honest,
It feels bitter-sweet to walk away from you.
Though I feel fulfilled knowing that we got to share souls as well as stories.
With that in mind, our story together isn't over.
We are still at the cover, and there are plenty of pages left to read.
So in our next tale,
I'll be sure to take my time.
And read very, very
Slowly.

"Nu-Your-E-Kin"

From the Motherland…
To this Island of Loneliness…
That's the Nuyorican.
Or New York Rican,
For those who aren't fluent in sexy.

A Puerto Rican poem is usually one of triumph and unity.
But today I am here to tell the story less told.
Because you need to call out,
The ones you love.

Our PR reps taught us to fit in with the lack of culture found in the United States.
Then we began to lose the language that was forced upon us by our previous landlords.
Those who lost that language, then had to master the parcel tongue needed to survive,
In this Land of Snakes.

From there, the very same people who taught you to be more them,
now get upset that you are more "them"
U.S.
Than us.
"Oo-ese"

The identity crisis continues when you have to choose between
the 'appeal' of the black struggle or,
the 'burden' of white privilege.
And for those who are *stubborn* enough to keep their own traditions in this grand flower pot,
They don't grow.

When it comes to race, we don't see Boricua on a form.
Instead, we are the fabled reptilians.
Our true race, the chameleon who has camouflaged ourselves into all walks of life.

Our Island is suffering.
And ironically so are the people who no longer live there.
So why did we leave?
Why do we stay?
When will we unite?
And when will we join our Latin American siblings,
hand and hand, judgment free and full of love?
Does Now work for you?

"Moving Day"

With tears in my eyes I packed up all my stuff, not knowing what I was walking away from. I wouldn't yet know what I'd be walking into. Most of my items, condensed into shopping bags that I would be lugging with me for the long ride home, *felt heavier than usual.* Whereas there would usually be this celebration of sorts and a lasting memory where you would get your proverbial flowers, this time I was lucky enough to get a few rosebuds, a pat on the back and the iconic "good luck with your future endeavors". "Yeah definitely, we'll be in touch", "We'll get together in a couple of weeks"! And what that really means is, sadly, we'll be losing touch indefinitely. So, as I reflected for all of those two stops into my long commute home, I knew then what I would come to find out very soon. This day would be the LAST day I would EVER live my life in comfort. I woke up to the weekend.

Anticipation, expectations, the prospect of new creations and new relations. The longest two days ever and yet, I kept my patience.

Monday comes! I pick my head up off the pillow; it's moving day. I grab the stuff I think I need. I make my way toward the door, out the house, to the train, and through the tunnels, only to resurface down this corridor of bricks and trees, encapsulated by a ceiling of sky. I follow the maze of misdirection, unaware at the time of the shortcuts that lead me to what I can only describe as… Wonderland?

Door opens… I step inside.

It's warm. It feels as if the rays of the sun were all bottled up. But I did not yet know where this energy was coming from. The one thing I did know however was that whatever feelings which existed in the outside world, did not enter with me… I was somehow somewhere else.

"Weary traveler, are you hungry?" I felt like I was at the start of a quintessential "hero's journey" and the thrill of adventure took over. I would go on to meet the source of this warmth, the living batteries that moved around this building, offering knowledge, wisdom, hospitality and a smile. From the youngest adult to the eldest child, I was welcomed. Usually I was the one who rolled out the metaphorical red carpet for others and I was labeled above and beyond for that. Here, I was just another face in the crowd and truthfully, I love it.

Then I would go on to meet the All-Stars who I would have the privilege of calling my team. Friday I was the "big dog". Monday, I'm the runt of the litter and I am blessed to have found my pack. Speaking of pack, I would begin to unpack my items, now as a minimalist placing down a cup which bears the first letter of my name. The day ends.

As I walk out of Wonderland, back into the world that you know, registering all that I just walked into. Everything that I just walked out of. A tear almost comes to my eye.

I feel lighter than usual.

Jay R. Midas Chapters [Transcribed]: Ch. 2.0 - 2.5*

jayrmidas.com

Chapter 1.0 *The Beginning is Present*

Chapter 1.5 *Detours and Destinations*

Chapter 2.0 *The Past is EterNaL*

Chapter 2.5* *future!TENSE.*

Chapter 3.0 *The Future is a 2nd Away*

Chapter 3.0.1 *The Future is a 2nd Away Act II*

Chapter 3.0.2 TFi2A Act II: *The NeedeRealm Trials*

Chapter 3.5 TFi2A Act II: *Dissent into 2088*

Chapter 4.0 *Convergence 2088*

Chapter 2.0 *The Past is EterNaL*
"Sitting in an Empty Room"
"Caught Up in the Rain"
"As I Think of You"
"Why?"
"The Eternal Struggle"
"This is how YOU Make Me Feel"
"Different Paths on the Same Road"
"Hold on to Your Dream"
"My Oxymoron"
"I'd Rather Be a Hero"
"A Wonder for the Future"

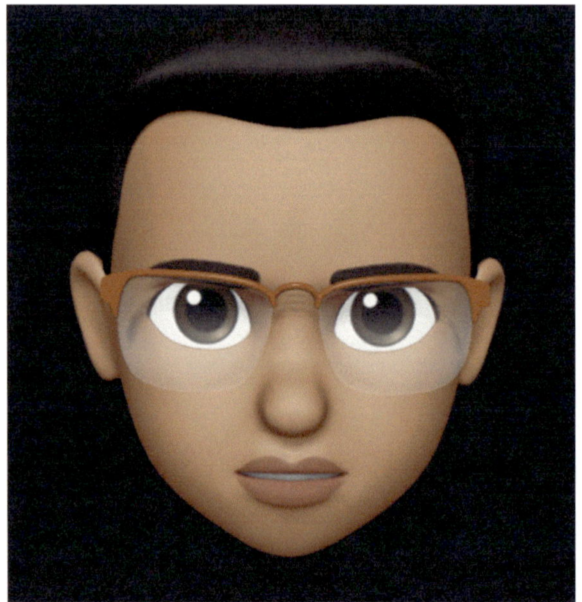

Back on schedule and during a period of reflection, Chapter 2.0 The Past is EterNaL attempts to answer the questions of teen melodrama and angst by reminding yourself that you were once unpolished, inexperienced and had a different set of priorities. Powerful words from a growing adolescent who could not yet fully grasp some of the concepts he touched upon. There is some accuracy within the inexperience that exists in this chapter. Whether stopping to feel the rain, sitting alone in silence, or your whole world ending because *the love of your life is an unrequited one*, a young Midas speaks to some universal truths that through age deepens wisdom. Mostly intact from source, some of the poems are gently modified with the painter's brush to revise the message, smoothen the lines or to demonstrate growth over time. Please enjoy what remains unchanged, **Chapter 2.0 The Past is Eternal**.

"Sitting in an Empty Room"

Sitting here in an empty room
Just thinking of you
I wish that you were here
But your not
So I can't help but shed a tear
Lost all my feelings physically
But emotionally a different story
You can't see the pain on my face
Because my mind is in another place
Significance of life is gone right now
Depression consumed me, how did I let it allow?
Life is the mixture of anguish and joy
Seems a bit one sided without life's glory

"Caught Up in the Rain"

Caught up in the rain/ Not going anywhere/ I put my bookbag down /and feel the refreshing air/ My body gets all wet/ But I don't give a damn/ For the first time in a lifetime/ I know who I am/ I take a breath, close my eyes and envision a girl I know/ I open my eyes and realize how much I care for her so[,]/ I can't stand here forever/ Pick up my bag and head toward the unknown/ My journey has just begun/ Tonight I'm not going home

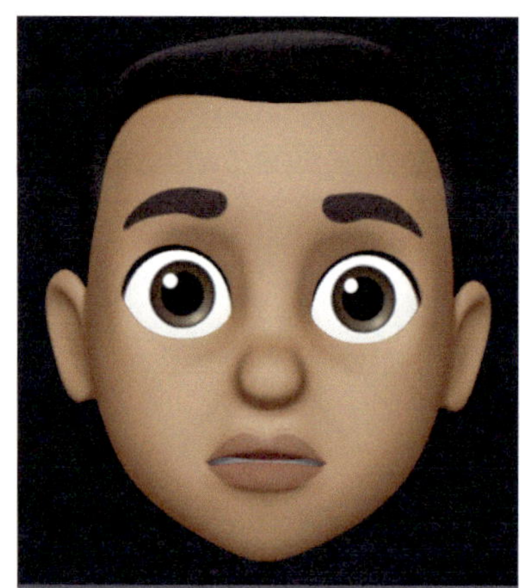

"As I Think of You"

I remember when I was lost in your eyes and never wanted to be found/ Now that you're gone, I miss you around/ Just when I thought that this was all finished/ My feelings for you never diminished/ Instead I miss you more everyday/ I now think of you while lying awake/ You are even in my dreams/ I believe it's a reality or so it seems/ When I awaken it gets me mad/ Because being here without you makes me sad/ I want these memories to reoccur, those dreams to come true/ Whatever the case is, I don't mind as long as it's with you

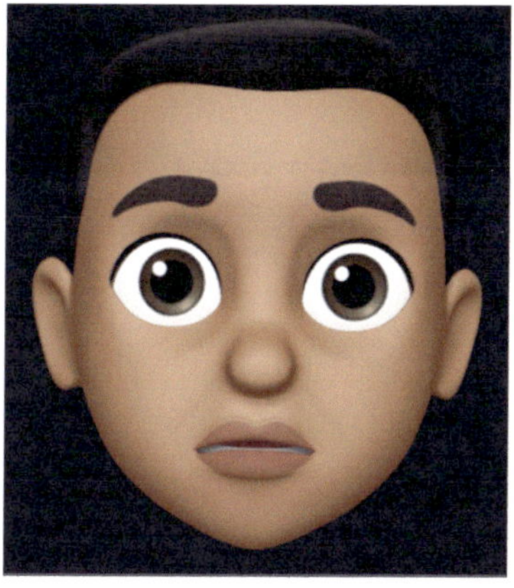

"Why?"

Why does it hurt?
Why do I care?
Why do I feel like I need you here?
Why do I cry?
Why do I think?
Why ask why for anything?
Why do I call and get no answer?
[Why], is it just me or is life a disaster?
I turned into something, I'd never be
I call for you at night in my sleep
I'm weak..I'm soft..I'm in love
But if I can't reach her, ~~than this poem isn't enough~~.
[Then I must unsee her, disappear, leave her
Because words are just not enough]

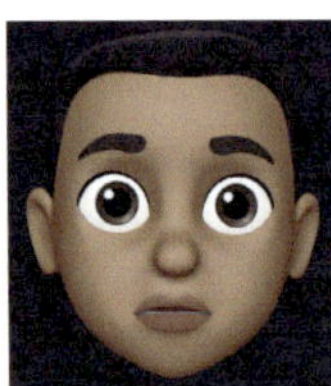

"The Eternal Struggle"

I live the eternal struggle
And I try to fight
I only try to take the path
That I ~~think~~ believe is right
Each and every step
I always seem to take
I walk into an obstacle
And ~~always~~ [find new ways] to make mistakes
I'm better off being the opposite
Of ~~what~~ who I'm supposed to be
I seem to have [enough] trouble
Just being me
~~Every decision I seem to make turns out wrong~~
The choices I've been making
Seem to turn out wrong
As if ~~this~~ life is predetermined
And I don't know what's going on
It plays with my mind
Til' I can't think
As if these problems
Are somehow linked
Then ~~there are~~ are the times
That ~~these~~ those problems get to me
Now it's time for me to open my eyes
And begin to see [with blind clarity]

"This is how **YOU** Make Me Feel"

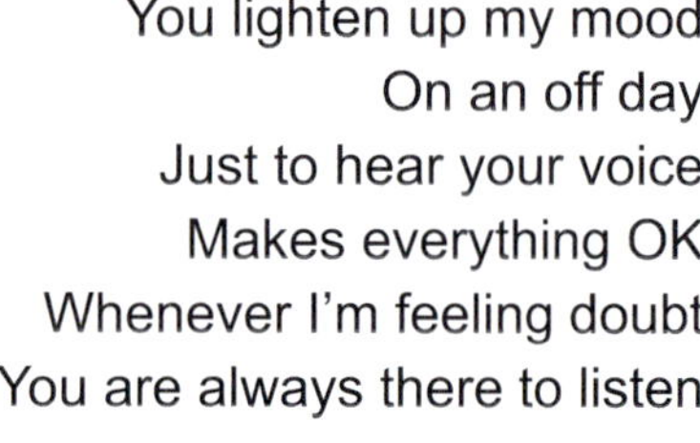

You lighten up my mood
On an off day
Just to hear your voice
Makes everything OK
Whenever I'm feeling doubt
You are always there to listen

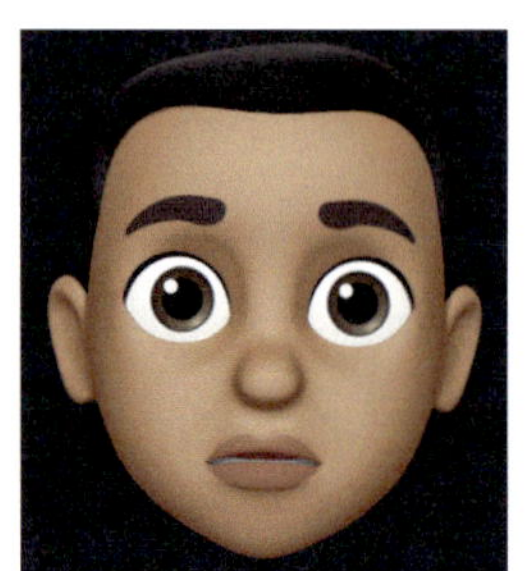

Thank you for hearing me out
And for trusting my decisions
You make me understand
What caring is all about
You always make me sure
Whenever I'm feeling doubt
I owe a lot of who I am to you
For [sharing laughs and] opening my eyes
Giving me peace of mind
[For waking me up, taking me in], and making me,
Me.

Signed,

J.Rodriguez

“Different Paths on the Same Road”

She’s carefree

He’s careless

She lives life for herself

He lives to make a mess

She experienced accidents

And he made mistakes

She learns to solve her issues

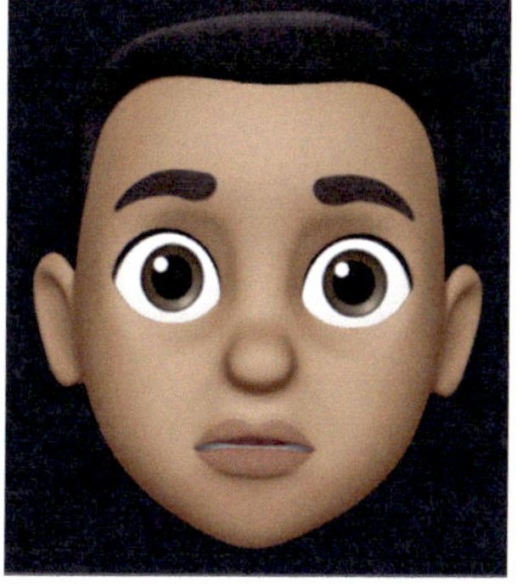

He says “life’s too hard to take”

She confronts her problems

As he stares his down

She does her best [to overcome]

And [somehow] his stay lingering around

But one thing he says

Is that he always does his best

Because in the name love

He withstands the rest

“Hold On To Your Dream”

You have a dream…
Something to hold on to
Something that keeps you sweet
Something that helps you be you
This would be the time to act upon your dream
You’d believe you’d see illusions
Or so it may seem
It’s a reality that you are well on your way
Let no one stop you
Keep going
Your goal takes more than mere days
Go, move on
Go with what you believe
Take any step
For your dream you shall achieve
This is YOUR dream
Do not go to sleep
You must act on it night and day
If your dream you intend to keep

"My Oxymoron"

You are my innocence
You are my guilt
You are the mixture of all emotions built
You are my gain
You are my loss
You are a combination of all lines crossed
You are my escape
You are my problems
But in the end
Things aren't fixed but you somehow solve them
You feel so right
And yet, so wrong
You my love are
My Oxymoron

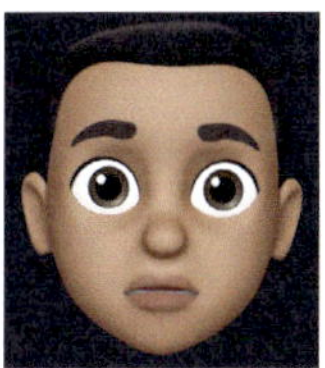

"I'd Rather Be a Hero"

I'd rather be a hero
My name etched in stone
Than a lonely lifeless zero
With a name unmade at home
I'd rather keep my dignity and be something more
So that people could get more of me
I just want to be adored
If I go out than I go out
I just want success
I do not want to scream and shout
And simply go depressed
I want to be looked up to
And make this name for Everyone
I don't want to live a lie, but the truth
For when my life is done

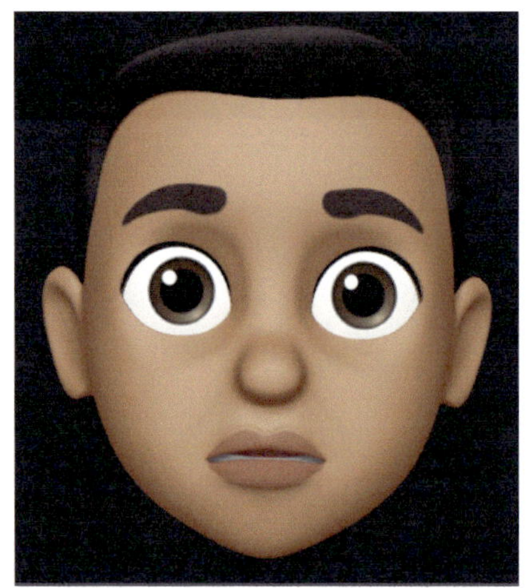

"A Wonder for the Future"

History is gone now
Now all etched in stone
Neanderthals, Cro Magnons
Are now all brittled bone
And as for the majestic creatures
That we call dinosaurs
We hear noise both far and wide
But we no longer hear their roar
Although we've gotten smaller framed
We call ourselves evolved
We've got cars, busses, trains and planes
Yet many problems left unsolved
According to the morning news
The present is bleak, dark and cold
Although world peace is hard to reach
It's unclear what the future holds
In this whole timeline of life
Who will take our place?
When it's finally our time to die
Who will ascend the human race?
Who or what
Will evolve from us?
Will it be a civilization free
Of hate and love?
Who knows what will happen
In the years to come
Hopefully life; humanity
Will learn to stand as one

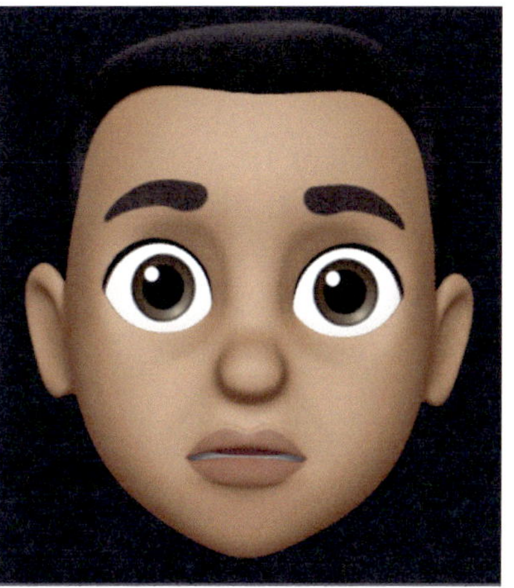

Chapter 2.5 (III) future!TENSE.
"Timeline Disturbance"
"Wair Duz"
"Filling"
"On the Other Side of A Black Hole"

Johnny Midas 2088 with Nola Sunglasses:

“Timeline Disturbance”

The Past and the Present have converged.

What does the Future hold?

Always on the brink of crisis.

But we see peace with half closed eyelids.

More worried about condemning decisions,

Than accepting their own

Change who they are are,

And yet somehow they've grown

Isn’t the true way to live,

To confront the unknown?

Welcome home.

“Wair Duz”

Where does (digital) technology come from? No, really?
Where does it come from?
And if you didn’t have access to technology, would you even know? No?
Where is this source of untapped, unlimited, electric energy?
And what equations using quadratic formulas, linear functions
and the negative square root of 3i,
Would have led us to accessing this energy that doesn’t seem to be,
Of our world.
A question that probably would have aroused Nikola Tesla.
Imagine, what fun he would have had with an mp3 player?
Do we really harness lightning energy?
If so, how?

Don’t Google it you dweeb!

Think,
Imagine,
Guess,
Discover,
Make the brain feel useful.
Has technology helped us or hurt us?
Yes.
We are now more united than ever.
We are more divisive than ever.
Do we really have a handle on the energy that we harness?
Do we really have a handle on ourselves?
Unplugging on Instagram, simply means you just went wireless
A child’s lesson teaches that everything has feelings
So, how have you treated Alexa lately?
Because apparently, she never forgets.
And,
Is it a coincidence that the modern version of the desktop computer was released
In 1984?

What was my initial question again?

Then again, don’t bother.

“Greetings from 2088”

It’s post-apocalyptic on this side of the timeline.
We’re really hurting out here and all we’re saying is I’m fine.
Unapologetic, over energetic.
Overeducated, underpopulated.
Maximize creators, minimize creations.
Scaling down the workforce,
Hiking up inflation.
This beats the evolution of humanity,
Can it be?
Harmony has yet to be achieved because of vanity.
Insanity, mother Earth is staring at us angrily.
We attempt to break her down, we’re doing it mechanically.
Organically, see beyond the vantage point the eyes can see.
The ones that rest beyond the lens outlook of divinity.
I love you to infinity.
That’s what life is like you see.
When we achieve some symmetry.
We have formed Affinity.

“Filling”

I’m showing fragments of greatness.
Trying to put these shards together that don’t seem to fit.
My wholeness is dividing.
My oneness has become lost in multiplicity
Justified by the one I can’t account for.

“On the Other Side of A Blackhole”

On the other side of a blackhole.
There I am, with you
And the world!
Exactly as we are now.
Nothing’s changed
Though everything is different now, right?
You’re part of it-
We’ve traveled endless light years, for stagnance!
Give or take,
You still will hold.
You never need ask for defeat.
When the highest currency is love.
In the eye of a blackhole, you’ll never see reality again!
Then return to your disbelief in the supernatural.

Jay R. Midas Chapters [Transcribed]: Ch. 3.0- 3.0.1

jayrmidas.com

Chapter 3.0 *The Future is a 2nd Away*
"Your Connection is Strong"
"Sleepless"
"Familiar"
"Let This Be the Intro Verse 1"
"Golden Boy Verse 1"
"Defeating Emotional Poverty"
"Love Poem for Poetry"
"The Face of God" (10 chosen lines from freestyled poem)
"Nourishment I Speak"
"Da Me Cafe"

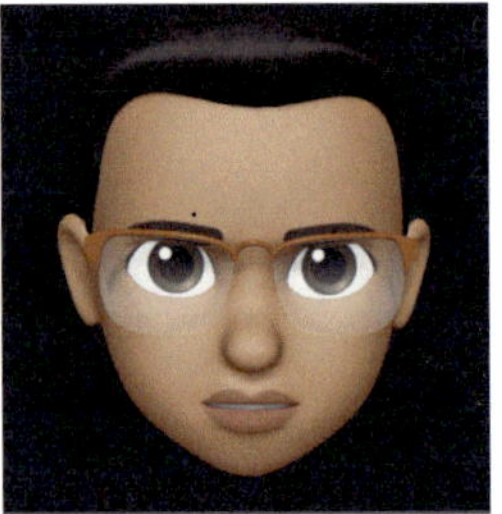

This is where poetry takes a full Sci-Fi turn for Jay R. Midas.

In contrast to previous chapters, stand-alone pieces as part of a cumulative project, Chapter 3.0 The Future is a 2nd Away bridges the previous chapters to create one expansive Poetry Adventure story across time; setting the evolution for the following chapters.

A variant Midas shows up suddenly to 2088 causing destruction in a distant future. *Mega Midas*, as he is called, is headed through various points in time to meet and eliminate different eras of himself for reasons which are still a mystery. Selected, "*Midi*" pulled from the timeline, must gather together to stop their opponent and preserve their existence in synchrony.

"Your Connection in Strong"

Your spirit.
Your body does work for your spirit.
Who do you give your spirit to?
What do you give your time to?
Where are the beneficiaries of my choices?
Who does the body want to represent?
We are all but mere angels who inherited *bipedal* mammals.
Exhilarated at the prospect of sacrificing it's only possessions;
Skin and Bone.
How do I become the person I always wanted to be overnight?
I just have to become it.
How do I make peace with the world around me?
Don't.
Simply allow the world to go to battle with itself,
Then call a truce for the war within yourself.

"Sleepless"

I used to rest easy, but now I can't sleep
Because you have only become a memory
You are no longer physical
But I know you're still here
I love you but you haunt me
You've become my [biggest] fear
Ever since your departure
All this you left behind
I don't know where you have gone,
Oh dear friend of mine
There is only one way
This pain will ever mend
I'm afraid to follow you where you have gone,
That's the only way we'll meet again.

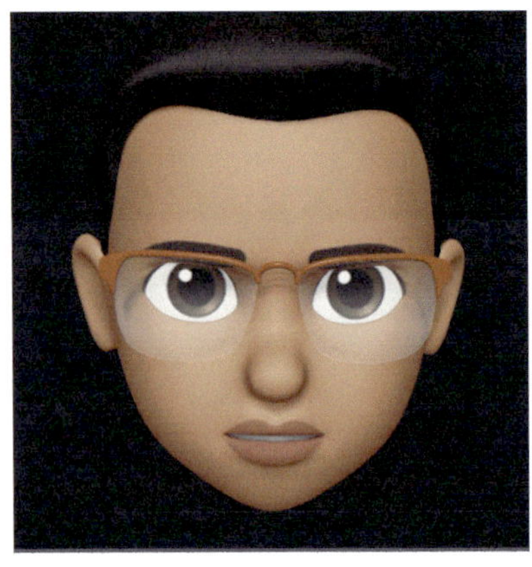
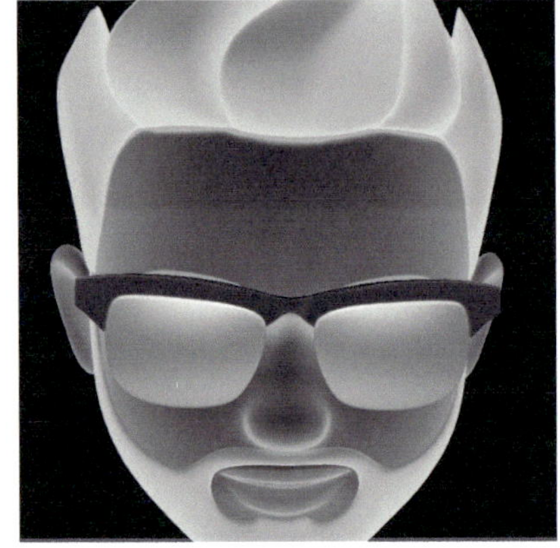

“Familiar”

In the time that we met, I feel like I’ve returned to a place I’ve never seen

I walk through this path as if I know where to go, perhaps it’s a dream

But can sense every taste, smell all the scents and get a chill from the touch

I know that I’m lost but I feel like I’m home so now I’m in flux

My thoughts might be scattered, my mind is a cloud, but I’m focused on you.

There are parts that I know, parts that are mysterious, but your eyes leave me clues

The one thing I know is that I’m unsure, but I live for the thrill

I want to resist, but as soon as I’m kissed, I succumb to your will

I’m out of my zone and into your world, allow me to travel

I’m entranced by your tale, please tell me more, let the story unravel

I want your time but you give me moments, I’m becoming obsessed

You hold me close but distance yourself, I admit I’m impressed

I don’t know where I’m going but I’ll find what I need with my heart as my compass

I’ll embrace your joy and take your pain and endure all your punches

As I walk through this world that is not of my own, it’s becoming much clearer

This is where I want to be, I’m moving here

Let’s get familiar

"Let this be the Intro" (Original Song by 'Jon E. Midas' First Verse)

Let this be the intro for the dearly departed,
The guys who got it started
And for those who weren't marketed

Toast to those who got it poppin',
Anticipated albums yet to be dropping

Big ups to the rappers who were one of a kind
The ones who tried their hardest but are yet to be signed

Hold ya head keep faith,
Move at a steady pace, make sure these execs don't forget a face

This is the advice I have to give to myself,
Am I doing it for the music, the fame, or the wealth?

A whole bunch of things come in to question,
But the answer becomes clear once my name is mentioned

Truth be told I'm was an egotistical guy,
When people heard me rhyme, it came as a surprise

Now all I do is smile,
I want to go from low key to high profile,
So, that's my style.

“Golden Boy”
Verse One
(2021)

I’m stuck between whether I want to fit in or stand out
“Stand down, stand down, man down”
I don’t know where I’m at,
I don’t know who I am
Am I pushing peace
Or do I give a damn?
About the things that are not me?
Or family?
My circle?
All closing.
Chorus: “I had to give up Midas in order to the Golden Boy…”

"Defeating Emotional Poverty" - Mantras

I had to know myself, say your mistakes out loud. [Identification]
Chances are if you don't want to hear it, it's the thing that needs to be addressed. [Acknowledgement]
You are going to fail every day, we can't live up to our expectations every time, be persistent. [Forgiveness]
Even the experts are wrong sometimes. [Inner-Trust]
The only person who can get me out of a hole is me. [Independence]
Not everyone goes with you on your journey, though try to bring people up. [Service]
You are more powerful than you **think** you are… You are more powerful than you **know** you are. [Spirit]
Make time for things that make you happy. [Self-Care]
It won't get done until you put in the work. [Accountability]
Make your expectations clear and honor your word. [Honesty]
Make allies on the come up, show them love. [Inclusion]
You are not going to agree on everything and some situations are down right fucked up, turn your pain into your passion. [Artistry]
Be intentional about your love, show love everyday to different people. The act of love will begin to diminish hate or negativity. [Growth]
People are going to make fun of what they don't understand. Greatness is a foreign concept to losers. Don't be a loser. [Self-Actualization]

Finish what you started,
Restarted what you finished
Loved me when I was gone
When I was there it had diminished
Kept me from being happy
But didn't stop me from being pleasured
You were always coveted
But you were never treasured
Until today…

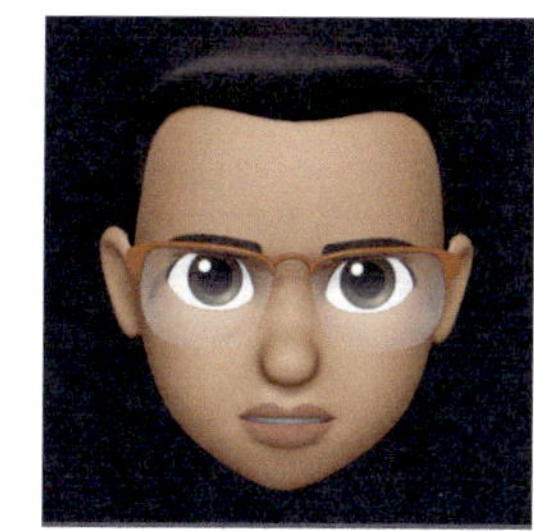

Love you Poetry <3

"Love letter to Poetry"

Dear words,

Always,
Midas

"The Face of God Freestyle" (10 Lines)

I. When you stare at the face of God, you stare at the face of God/ Another human feels less important/ Should it be the other way around?....
II. ...Make time for the light, make time for the darkness, make time to address the things that give you bliss
III. ...the things that make you better, the things that make you thrive, instead of a collective hive mind, where an individual's thoughts *is* an afterthought...how much havoc have we wrought on ourselves, I don't know.
IV. ...they always leave you to sweat, because they will leave you in regret, making a choice that you knew was right, and you when it was time to fight, they would eat you because they have the appetite, and they will try to throw your name in the mud because they think it's right. They don't realize how much they are out of sight
V. ...But I have to love this place, but as I had said previously you have to call out the ones you love, and in this particular case, that's you, you call me out all the time, so it's my turn, it's time that you learn, I love you too
VI. We could always change the game, when we change the value, when we change the currency, so let's change the currency allow people to be talented to be talented...smart...bright and lively and happy in this country... and the values will double and triple...B!!!!!!!!!!!
VII. When you live in the mind of God your heart begins to open, your heart begins to open
VIII. You get ready to help the people you love and the ones you will meet along the way, yo, journey going to be sweet they say
IX. Don't forget to advocate for what's right in your heart, don't forget to advocate for what's right from the start
X. On the journey whether you are wrong or your right, always root for justice and peace, always root for justice and peace, always root for justice and peace

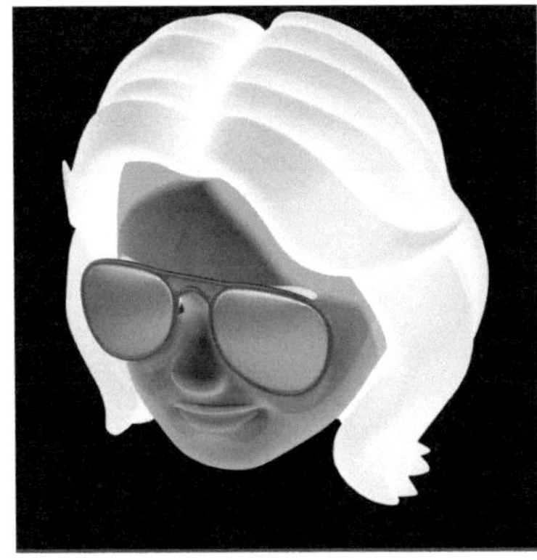

"What I feed off is my nourishment"
Toxicity comes in the flavor of menthol
The truth is too bitter
A lie is too sugary
A fact is too bland
An opinion is too sour
Information is too grainy
Hope is too light
Despair is empty calories
Criticism is too sharp
Hate tastes rotten
Depression is too fattening
Confusion is the sensation of cottonmouth
Love tastes like Bourbon maple syrup
Variety must be Adobo
Stimulation is so savory
Friendship is umami
Condescension remains tasteless
Gossip is too creamy
Fear tastes spoiled
Support is such a delicious pastry
Wisdom is so filling
People seem to love delicious poison
Reality is so flavorful

"Da Me Cafe"

What I'm saying is I love you, "Da Me Cafe"

I wouldn't be where I am without you, "Da Me Cafe"

You been there for me at times when I have been at my lowest, "Da Me Cafe"

I wish I could have treated you better, when you have been so good…to me, "Da Me Cafe"

I would have loved to meet your every desire, but there wasn't enough overtime I could work that could afford our security, I'm sorry, "Da Me Cafe"

Yes, I've loved other women, no none of them were you, I can't put into words how special you are to me, "Da Me Cafe"

You are the very reason I could say I'm proud of the family we created, "Da Me Cafe"

I could have pulled my weight more when raising the kids, "Da Me Cafe"

I wish I didn't let my vices get in the way of our happiness, "Da Me Cafe"

When I couldn't breathe, and I could no longer walk the same, you were my air and my legs, "Da Me Cafe"

The seeds of generational Puerto Rican success, began with our union,

"Da Me un Beso".

Chapter 3.0.1 *The Future is a 2nd Away Act II*
"Natural Anomaly"
The "Monologue"
"Nolito's Rules"

March 2023

A poetry tale with the feel of an expansive RPG, the story continues to progress and evolve. As of January 2024, the current story is ongoing and the big showdown between Midas' across time is happening live in the year 2088- **Chapter 4.0** *Liberation 2088 Battle Zone!* There will only be one remaining… For now, I shall leave you at TFi2A Act II. It is a shorter chapter that focuses on more quality and succinct delivery and is the part of the story where the other shoe drops from a storytelling lens. The aftermath of a confrontation leads both sides to change up their strategies. One side reshuffles the chess pieces, the other side takes the strategic, "divide and conquer" approach. The themes of this Chapter include maturity, betrayal and shifting dynamics. "Natural Anomaly" serves as the setting which sets the stage for the crescendo of the poetry adventure story. The written version focuses on the letter "A" to demonstrate how often, yet rarely the letter shows up. *The* "Monologue" is a literal and ironic title because the Antagonist of the story is attempting to convince his most competitive rival to join him, which in many ways is him. But not. When you know yourself so well, does that make you easier to convince? The plot continues to thicken in the subsequent **TFi2A Chapter 3.0.2** *The NeedeRealm Trials*, **Chapter 4.0** *Liberation 2088*, then briefly stepping back to **TFi2A Chapter 3.5** Dissent into 2088 before wrapping up the story.

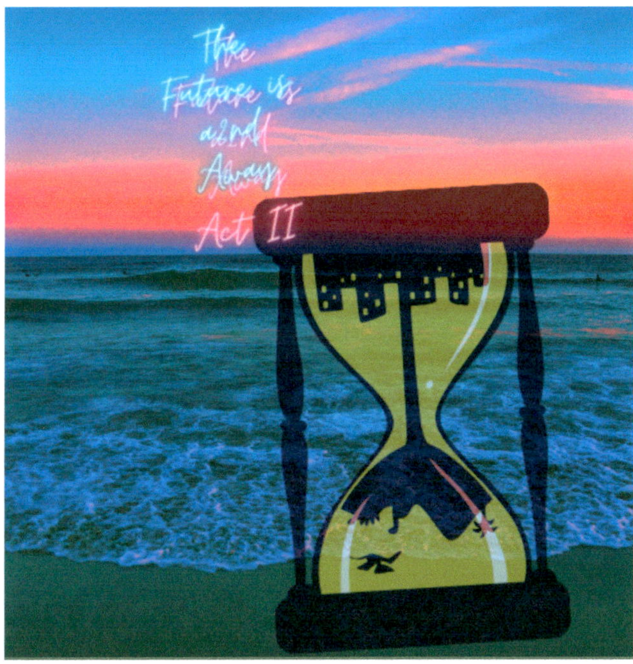

"NAturAl AnomAly"

On the rooftop, the sound of A motorcycle. The sight of A helicopter in the sky moving At the speed of stillness. The breeze of A plAstic bAg flies under A sunny sky. Supersonic movement of A domestic plAne disturbs the bird's errAtic flight pAtterns. Chirping, the pigeons begin to get competitive. HumAnity's vAlue is bAsed on skill. A being's skill is regArded through opportunity. The decibel of A bAby's cry reminds us thAt Answers Are not usuAlly presented on time. A new tune blAres out of the window of trAnsportAtion, the sound creAtes three new fAns. Only to-dAy's left. A new sky.

***The* "Monologue"**

"The world is spiraling, you see that now... and you're spiraling with it. I'm from the timeline where you didn't experience a global event. In the time you were locked down, my life went on. The blurred lines of order, power, and quality living were revealed to you in a way it wasn't to myself...At least not immediately. In many ways you have it harder, in others you have it much simpler. But let me tell you something, whatever path you take, you have shown resilience. You know the outcome now. You know how the story plays out. Isn't it better to have you on this side? To prevent you from making the wrong decision... again? You have the rare opportunity of saving yourself, by force if necessary. I don't stand here today as opposition, but as your biggest asset. These are the very same glasses you walked down Bourbon St., from 65+ years into the future. Supercharged. So grab your destiny, take charge, and save yourselves. The world...is on its own."

Nolito's Rules:

1. I operate by the rules of the Golden Affirmations
2. I seek to emit positive energy

3. I seek to attract positive energy
4. I will disrupt negative energies
5. Family flows through me, all qualities. Always choose the wisest path.
6. Confront opposition head on.
7. Convene with my council and align with their united decision.
8. Money is a mode of transportation, it's not the warm embrace of a loved one.
9. Forgive, always forgive. When you cannot forgive, you must avenge.
10. Love is mutually beneficial without having to ask for anything in return.
11. When yeses and no's are final answers, ask why?
12. Keep focused on the priority, and putting the pieces back together is the priority.
13. Ignore the creatures of the night, they will only get you in trouble.

Jay R. Midas Chapters [Transcribed]:
Ch. 3.0.2- 3.5

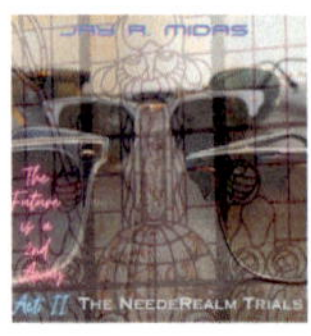

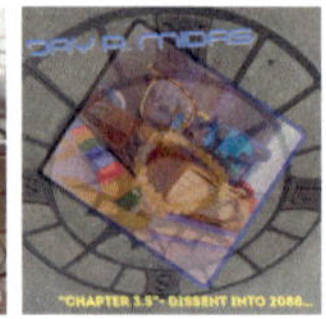

jayrmidas.com

Chapter 3.0.2 TFi2A Act II: *The NeedeRealm Trials*
"Rough Draft Thought"
"Lineage"
"Rando's Reality"
"Anger is.."
"My Ology"
"Heartz N' Spadez"

The continuation of ***Chapter 3.0.1 The Future is a 2nd Away Act II,*** *Mega Midas, Rockstar Jon E. Midas and Rando all venture to the NeedeRealm for this sidequest adventure which has major implications over the main story. A new character is introduced that may tip the scales of balance back into the favor of Team Rando (Rando, BB Wayz and Midas 06'). This mini-chapter features quick hitting one-punch poetry and acts as the springboard directly into Chapter 4.0 Liberation 2088. This story also runs concurrently with* ***Chapter 3.5 Dissent into 2088.*** *Featured poetry in this chapter are "The Rough Draft Thought", "Hardship", and "Heartz n' Spadez".*

"The Rough Draft Thought"

The rough draft thought is messy
It needs the pencil's greatest gift
The erasure
Saying what you need to say
Isn't as easy
As saying what you need to say
That's the unfortunate get dumped
Fired
Hurt
and Broken
...The caveat...
Mindfulness is a maze
A labyrinth
A trap if you let it
Miles completed within minutes
Major milestones make for monumental moments
Try to trick your thoughts to take a back seat to your actions
Acting too fast is a role that we are all destined for
The absence of critical thinking leads to criticism
The act of constant care to correct creates chaos within the cranium
Experience allows for few mistakes
And the ability to laugh off the ones we make
The child and wisdom
Both of which are never fake
The openness to grow and create
The only we lie is when we go to sleep
So we don't end up lying awake

"Lineage"

I've housed a menagerie of fear within the catacombs of my memories. I'm from a warrior species and we stopped fighting long ago. Now today's most ferocious opponent is mental illness. Peace and resonance is an act of the will.

"Rando's Reality"

Head up, Chest out

Slouching is an exercise in laziness

Depression is a nap for the uninspired

Fake it til' you make it or keep it real to the top

Does the method matter when achieving your defined success?

After you expire, you stop writing your story to become a tall tale.

I want to look back on my life not wanting to have to apologize for my existence.

You choose to ignore people who will remember you best.

But you sacrifice time with them, for them.

That's deranged.

Save family, save motivation, spend motion.

The direction is forward.

The path is straight.

And unity is now.

For if not.

It never existed.

"Anger is"

Anger is an unhandable truth that comes to the surface at a time when we're not ready to face it. You live in fiction when you can handle all the things put in front of you.

"My Ology"

Challenge my ism, update my ology, erase my phobia and make me whole.
Stand in silence, grace behold.

2 of a kind, Ace high, You and I bay-beh.
"Heartz and Spadez"

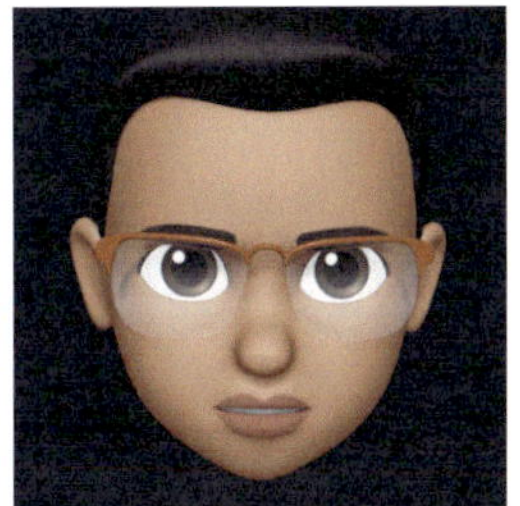

Chapter 3.5 TFi2A Act II: *Dissent into 2088* (Story Driven Side Quest)
"Certificate of Deposit "
"Times Square Light Show" (Chorus)
"Epiphany"

Chapter 3.5 is the era yet to be seen!

As the contestants in the big Poetry battle of 2088 gear up for the big encounter, Team Rando and Team Mega Midas work on their final preparations. This chapter is special because it features other characters than Jay R. Midas. We take a leap in time to find out what happened with BB Wayz and Midas 06'. When Rando, Jon E. Midas and Mega Midas were all training and had their run in during **Chapter 3.0.2 The NeederRealm Trials**, concurrently BB Wayz and Midas 06' are fending for themselves in the distant future in **Chapter 3.5 Dissent into 2088**. Featured poetry in this chapter include "Certificate of Deposit" and bytes like "Times Square Light Show", and "Epiphany".

I can't always give money
Please use my gems
I can share my time with you
But I need time too
So even if now is not the time
Even now, you are on my mind
In my thoughts
Tethered to my essence
Thank you for providing me
Company
In solitude
"Certificate of Deposit"

"Times Square Light Show (Song Chorus)"

Times Square light show

Millionaire bankroll

Money is funny, man

That's the way the Game goes

Swimming & Women and a whole lot of cash flow

I followed the lights, now follow me

Where I go.

Epiphany.

Woke up.

Good as new.

More grown than yesterday.

But I still remain youthful

I don't need to feel inspired.

Just need to know who I am.

Where I have been and where I'm headed

I have become the very fabric of life itself

This is who I have always been nevertheless.

This is who I have been more or less

I have become the very fabric of life itself

Where I have been and where I'm headed

Just need to know who I am

I don't need to feel inspired

But I still remain youthful

More grown than yesterday

Good as new

Woke up

Epiphany

Jay R. Midas Chapters [Transcribed]: Ch. 4.0

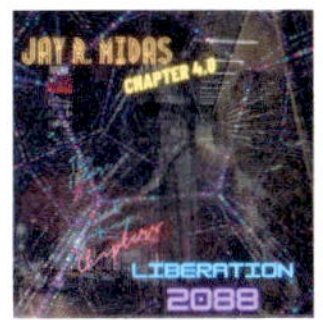

jayrmidas.com

Chapter 4.0 *Liberation 2088 (Pre-Showdown)*

"Pipe Dream"

"Color"

"Ignorance Sq.(uare)"

Chapter 4.0 *Convergence 2088 (Battle Episodes)*

"Kiss the Lips of Fiction" -Ep. 12

"Stupid' -Ep. 12

"Mirrors" -Ep. 13

"Lonely" -Ep. 13

"The Late Comer" -Ep. 14

"No 2.0" -Ep. 14

"Reddish and Bloosie" -Ep. 15

"Jay R. Midas"

"Let it All Go" -Ep. 19

"Know Who I Am" -Ep. 20

"Shattered Intersectionality" -Ep. 21

"Times Square Lightshow Remix" -Ep. 22

"Distortion Perfection" -Ep. 23

Readings from Golden Affirmations -Ep. 24

"What's in a Name aka Good-Will" Ep. 26

"Life" Ep. 27

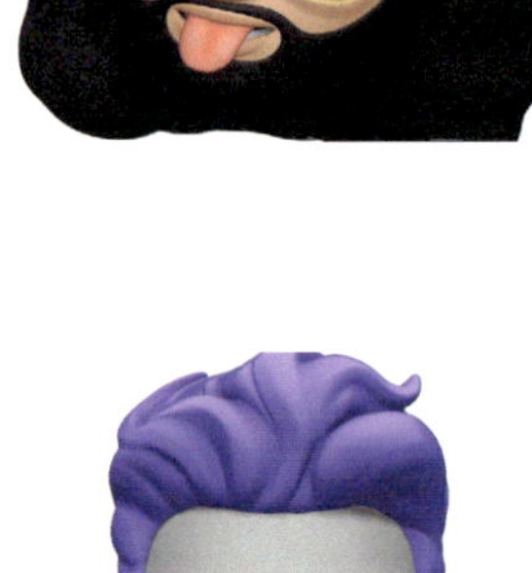

~~"The Dead Seed" Ep. 29~~ Refer to Chapter 5*

BONUS- "My Life as a Battery Powered Yo-yo…

"The Naysayer" Ep. 34

"No Kaep" Ep. 34

"The Algorithm" Ep. 35

"Sure" Ep. 35

"Ny" Ep. 36

"Nola. Pt. 2- The Other Side" Ep. 36

"Letter to Leon" Ep. 38

"Freedom" Ep. 39

"Baby Blue Wayfarers" Ep. 41

"Golden Boy" Chorus Ep.43

"Consensus" Ep. 44

The Culmination of Chapter 3.0 The Future is a 2nd Away. There is nothing left to do but to battle it out and see who controls the trajectory of Midas' timeline.

"Pipedream"

I'm famous and I'm the only one who knows it
I may never walk across the stage of MSG, whatever own it
The path I walk is solitary but I'm never actually alone
The team is always with me, through the support that they have shown
I take my time on the come up, it's not worth the pain to rush
Because when you take no prisoners, you have to execute through touch
Instead, I hold no one hostage,you're exactly who you would like to be
That's what makes you, you and that's what makes me
I've been stepped on and stepped over
Look past, and lept over
No hostility left over, instead I stand bolder
Hoisting boulders over both shoulders
You can't stop me now when I'm superimposed in a pullover
Holding a four leaf clover
Because you need luck to swim against the current as you get older
Grow colder with the cold shoulder
It's over
Closure
Pipedream.

Who are you when the pressure is on?
Are you a diamond or are you dust?
Are you strong like steel or are you stuck like rust?
And after the shock, tears and oh woah is me,
Once the grief has passed, what do you see?
Do you get ready to rise and grind,
or do you let yourself fall behind?
Jealousy, struggle, anger and pain
Are all ingredients for going insane
But before you carve out a slice of that pie,
Know that the flavor is humble, your intolerant, you could die
When you find out that you're not the one
Do you keep on pushin' or are you done?
Too many players in an overcrowded game
Remove the cartridge, it's time for change
My cut is polished
My clarity is knowledge
My carat is nutrition
For my eyes are the vision, who am I?
I am,

"Color"

"Ignorance Sq.(uare)"

Next stop!
Insecurity
Eye to eye with the self
Seeing only what is
Is the shell empty?
Or does it house a tortoise with a long journey ahead
The ocean is still
The breeze is calm
Where to next?
Ignorance Sq.
Overpopulated,
Many move away
Last stop!
Wondercliffs
Watch the gap
This is the last ride back tonight
Express to Origin Parkway
Stand clear of the closing doors please!
Bing-Bong

“Kiss the Lips of Fiction”

Go ahead, lean on a shoulder.
That just shows you haven’t gotten older.
Your dependence for attention is do damn apparent
I could see right through you, you are so transparent
Now go ahead get a pen, take proper dictation.
Because one day will come a time for explanation.
Now do what you want for it will come right back.
It will pierce through your skin, sharp as a tack.
If you're getting afraid, it means I’m doing my job.
I’m getting through to that simple mind, and that takes a lot.
But!
Just because I say these words, doesn’t mean you listen.
I know you’re afraid of the truth, so kiss the lips of fiction.

"Stupid"

I'm not afraid to look stupid.
The pitfalls others avoid are my opportunities.
Intelligence is appearance.
Who has home field advantage in this conversation?
I'm not afraid to play away games.
The incessant need to be right was our original Bubonic Plague.
The fact that others have to subscribe to our opinions,
and the fact that we place our morals and ethics into another body,
reveals the biggest confliction life has to offer.
I've had the most effective responses,
and went with the wrong answers.
Because I was afraid of feeling-
Stifled...
Unheard...
Stupid.

"Mirrors"

All I see are mirrors.
Reflections of my mistakes staring back at me.
Although my strength is doubled
In your presence, I'm no longer what I see in those reflections.
I'm better now.
But better isn't my best.
And my mirrors are far from my worst.
Those cracked and broken glass fun house structures
Were tossed a long time ago
I see aspects of myself in the flesh and bone,
Blood and brain.
Those vanities carry daily.
My soul has been touched by countless lives
I see myself in your features
Hope you can see yourself in me too.

10/4/03

"Lonely"

The lonely boy wants his love
The girl that he's been dreaming of
He daydreams of the girl who makes him smile
And he knows she'll make it all worthwhile
He wants her to be a part of his life
Someday take his hand in marriage and be his wife
He's so in love, he believes he's indebted in heart
The boy keeps dreaming and then it starts
The boy snaps out of it and wakes up just to see
These visions he's been having make him more lonely.

"The Late Comer"

Okay, Okay don't be nervous.
Ring the doorbell and smile
Though not too much to the point where people think your strange
A cool smile
But not too cool
You don't want to come off as arrogant
There's going to be a lot of people here tonight
And All it takes is one
To ruin your [fucking] night.
And I could just very well be that one.
Sincerely hope not
I've been known to lose my cool once or twice
But no, **deep breath**
Positive vibes, gentle energies.
You're going to be the life of the party... no, the event!
Nah, that's too BIG time.
Just fit in and have a good time.
But I was told, not just to fit in,
But to stand out, right?
Or...or...or...
I could just go in and have fun!
Have fun...
Okay, okay don't be nervous.

"No 2.0"

Let's Begin...

Broken down to be rebuilt, there is no 2.0. All the feelings of survivors guilt, now the seedlings have to grow. I spent a thousand lifetimes in silence and loved the peace in there. Until I met myself straight up and learned I was self-impaired.

At First...

I pondered nurture. The genetic makeup of my conflictions. One side the calculated hand of Scorpio, the blind ambition of Pisces at its juxtaposition.

Needless to Say...

This Leo became split into a Gemini somehow, I walked down this path of purpose that leads me here and now.

This Just in...

Violence is always in the present and apparently so am I, so every moment I'm not entrenched in combat, it's a blessing in disguise.

Between Us...

When I'm not as right as I think I am, take the love and advice from others. Though I have gained complete trust in myself, so let's see what life uncovers.

Truth be Told...

I'm genetically designed to fail... Because that's how winners are made.
I took some bumps and got back up and pushed past being afraid.

Penultimately...

I learned a major lesson. Destiny is a string of actions.
The creators' plan superseded mine but you don't see it as it happens.

Finally...

As I reach the apex of this mountain, it's now time for us to part.
As you mind find when you look behind, I pull you back to start.

"Reddish and Bloosie"

Red or Blue? Dot. Dot. Dot. Classic question.
Reddish is the older sibling and if Reddish could talk, he would tell you about my bad parenting skills. Then she came. Bloosie.
The younger of the two. Spry and full of [battery] life.

Reddish is the handsome workhorse. I have all my serious conversations with Reddish. While baby Bloosie has all the fun. When I had lost my cool, I took it out on Reddish a couple of times. Never on Bloosie.

Bloosie is a good little sister though. Always finds Reddish when he gets lost. Reddish is not always so good at finding Bloosie. Reddish most times, relishes in silence. Bloosie is more concerned with who likes her.

Reddish feels neglected, Bloosie loves her independence. Reddish is the DJ. Bloosie is the photographer in the family. As I look into Reddish's eyes, as Reddish takes a peek into my lens...

The inevitable question of any multi-child parent is, who is the favorite? The answer is almost always the same... the youngest. But the oldest has the highest ceiling for making a parent proud and yes, it is true- Reddish is now fully mature, past the prime of life and Bloosie is living out her best years, looking fully mature in a very different aspect. Her capacity is now almost full.

The question on everyone's mind: "Reddish you are unlocked and past contract age, now what?"

[Reddish Speaks to the Crowd]

"I'm going to have the best conversations for as long as I am able".

R.I.P Reddish

“Self-Titled”

Joy is the key to happinesS
All alone at the top alphA
Yield to a legenD
Rise up to the exotic AçaI
Most don't prep for the storM
It's fruit bearing laboR
Don't think it comes easY
Although I'm a titan in this arenA
Shine brighter than your morniN' OJ.

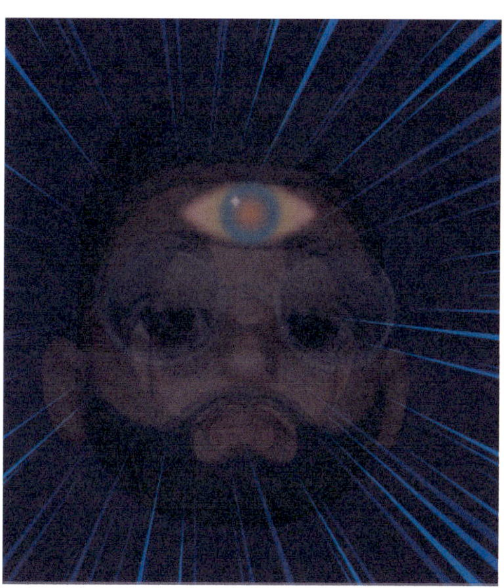

What's my name?

"Let it All Go"

I let it go.
All of the angst and the blame.
The misguided relationship dynamics.
I'm solemn on my knees ripping up the paper.
Telling myself, get it right for once.
Get it right the first time.
Mistakes.
I'll trade those in for gems of wisdom.
Irreversible damage, irrefutable changes.
I have released it all through my pores like perspiration.
Then the rain came...
The snow fell...
The moon lit...
The son rose...
Now I emit...
Light.

"Know Who I Am" - Verse 1 & Chorus

I could tell you,
How much of a struggle that its been
I could tell you,
How we lost so many friends.
I could tell you.
How we want this shit to end.
I could tell you,
We will never love again.
How many times were you criticized?
When you were hungry,
How many times were you fed lies?
Each time it felt like you died inside.
And you had to be the pheonix to spread the ashes and rise.
Why?
We say that we will be there every step of the way.
Only when things go well is what we neglected to say.
People who were once friends became enemies.
Friends become acquaintances partially by me.
This isn't an honest world
So who are we to trust?
Stop it with the puzzles, I think enough is enough.
I'm sick of confusing love for lust.
One thing I know is I'll never give up. What?
I'll live my dream...
This world unseen...
And I'll make sure you will know who I am...
Just to be heard...
If just one word...
Then I'll make sure...
You will know who I am.

"Shattered Intersectionality"

How much responsibility do I bear?
For being-
Puerto Rican
American
Male.
A New Yorker.
Party-Aligned
Independence,
With pre-conditions,
Ambitions
And hopes for a future.
But.
War is a love language
Technology is a lifeform

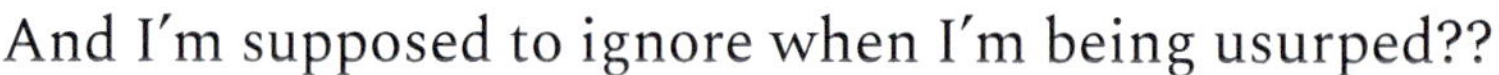
And I'm supposed to ignore when I'm being usurped??
Though, we remain unfooled.
Because we remain curious,
Over the proud
Many,
Who choose to be decisive.
There are no right answers.
Just feel right
When you have to answer for them.

Love,
aMEerica

"Times Square Lightshow Remix" -Verse 1 & Chorus

Money's the objective and I put it in perspective, waiting for my moment because I know I'm going to get it. Quit is not a word in my vocabulary. So I looked up another word in the Dictionary. Determination is what it's taking, you're mistaken if I'm breaking there's no time I could hardly sleep. This rockstar lifestyle always parties, always people as long as I'm standing on my feet. This is the...

Times Square light show

Billionaire bankroll

Money is funny, man

That's the way the Game goes

Swimming n' Women and a whole lot of cash flow

I followed the lights, now follow me

Where I go.

I'm in party mode, ready to let it go. Suited up like I was on duty but I'm about to steal the show. Stacking up cash cause' we are past the point of class. This is graduation, completed all of the tasks. I'm the bad guy with a good eye for scoping the baddest chick in the place. 10 minutes will be gone without a trace, can't wait to touch base. The only goal is to get home safe and I won't be late. Party on 42nd, bottles on deck. Middle of the square as we are looking to get wrecked. I was born ready- on your mark, get set, go! This is the Times Square light show. It's that kinda night when we hit up the Ave, this is our city so take what you can grab. Pockets deeper than the Grand Canyon, when it's all said and done we'll disappear like phantoms.

[Chorus]

"Distortion Perfection"

The sky is green
The oceans are yellow
Clouds are pink
And people are colorless
Physical touch reaches beyond the axis
Of the equator
Sound is visible
As streaks of aqua blue carry
Only to fall to the ground 30 feet away
Thoughts are tangible as they fill the space
That exits the mind of the creator
The mind has a location too
It's embedded deep inside the synapses of the stomach
Eyes are simply the limbs of the imagination
Light is the music of a heavenly song.

Action.

Excerpts from Golden Affirmations

“I am being of fire and water. Both of these entities fight for dominance within me. When I try to appease my flame [in liquid] it extinguishes itself. But if I could control the fire, the water then, the water, the fire then I am a being of the elements. Especially the element of surprise”.
We live in a cyclical system of perception.
Turn your fear into your fire.

"What's in a Name" aka GoodWill

- *Dedicated to Big Bro*

What's in a name? Is it letters comprised of vowels and consonants, that sum up syllables, that become nouns, that make up a person? Then it's the actions of that noun that determine whether one remains human or whether they become vermin or sea urchin?

But not you.

When life got hard you became a mountain. When the wells dried up you became a fountain. You made sense of the numbers and kept on counting on yourself, to have what it takes to keep on amounting to something. To have the iron will, the willpower, the presence of will which helps prevent the foundation of will from crumbling.

Opposers step forward stumbling and bumbling in the light of you. Mongers of fear cower at the sight of you and may that protective helmet you carry be the instrument that empowers that fight in you. May the right in you guide others to do what they know they have the right to do. And through your action others will be inspired too. Be who you were meant to be.

All it takes is a gesture of GoodWill.

"Life"

Life is comprise
Something to live by
With all the choices
We can't help but question why
Life cannot have good
Without the bad
Because how do we know if we're happy
If there is no sad
Life is free will
Freewill to do what we please
It's Our choice to look toward the sky
Or to get down our knees
Life is wisdom
The more we go through
The more we know
The power to change the bad in us
And have another side to show
Life is impulse
To act on how we feel
To discount what is fake
To point out what is real
And here I now stand
The narrator of this page
My name is Jay R. Midas
And I am all the *RAGE**

**Real Artist Group Entertainment- RAGE (Inactive)*

BONUS POEM: see Ch. 5 (coming soon to print) for Dead Seed

""My Life as Battery Powered Yo-yo, Fueled by Anger"

I took a good look at my life and realized I'm farther away from happiness than I've ever been. My mom needs to retire with safety and security knowing that everything will be taken care of. I'm sick of explaining my position to people who don't truly value my position. I am beginning to attract the eyes of my doubters. My smile is too bright, people are casting shadows, coasting in the shade. Joy for me is a lunch break. I served people with agendas while distancing myself from people who loved me unconditionally. It's okay though, it's a reminder to myself that complacency is one step closer to death. Consistent anger is too but at least I die doing something. If these be the last words I mutter, let these people who don't have my gift try to fill the void of my silence. A message to the manipulators and users, you are losers. No matter how successful you claim to be, know you get no respect from me. Like and subscribe.

I'm detached from this plane. The body still functions. The mind remains active, though my emotional epicenter is unphased by external catastrophe. My emotions have previously bounced up and down on a string like a yo-yo. Now the wiring is knotted although the yo-yo still looks intact because it was rewound meticulously. It looks as good as new. But don't try to use it. Best left in a display case, for viewing pleasure only. I require no interaction. Thrown into a collection, I now take on a vintage value so as not to depreciate, I must appreciate the depths of my anger as my battery to *'walk the dog on these bitches'*. Now bounce for me.

"The NAYSAYER"

Nay I say.
I say nay.
Look there may be another way.
Yes, that's great mate.
Don't be late
"Oh, I like change
But I won't wait"
The nuisance
The opposer
Gets trapped in their enclosure
When the Battle's won
The work's just begun
Let's work toward getting over...
The past
Nay.
Nay I say.
I say nay.
To build toward tomorrow
Focus on today
I know not what lies ahead
Although I'm well aware
Exactly what could happen
If I'm caught unprepared
Nah.
I'll even slack my jaw
To let y'all know not happening
Instead I'm grappling
Do I let things go?
Or double down?
With my head in the clouds
I stand my ground.
Lay low
It's time to grow
Up I go
You pushed to far
When I say no.
I am the Naysayer
And I will put a stop to those stifling progress.

Now, what do you do with your time left?

Fingertips on your soul, losing control, with half of your mind left

Looking to do right

battery low, nowhere to go

feeling so uptight

Righting a wrong, then moving on, such has been this life

The choice to do good, under the hood,

you know if you could

you'd be leading a bad life

The worry is being put in a bad light

Looking shady under the spotlight

Kicking things down, when no one's around

keeping it locked tight

Your free now

but what will you be now

taking a knee under them hot lights

A day ago everything was alright

"No Kaep" *- Title*

None at all.

Suffice to say, standing up for self, is in itself, dare I say, a sacrifice.

"The Algorithm"

You've been calling on me to save the algorithm, the millions of views that break the internet are curated for you. It keeps your range of focus predictable. Capable of making the same mistakes over again. Getting into the same arguments, over again. There are alot of things that happened that cannot be taken back. It's up to us to push it forward. In a horrible world, we are all horrible people. It's the perception but it's not the reality. We cannot speak for any other nation but we can speak from experience when I say coming form a world of difference, we all have much in common. Our values. It's okay to be an "alpha" because our world needs it. It's okay to be an outcast, because our world needs it. It's okay to be honest and disagree because you and I need it. But if we can find it in our hearts to do without so much of the rat racing, dog fighting and the cat and mouse games that we play, perhaps, we increase our quality of life just a bit, enough to the point where we recognize that there is more than there is 2 opinions on things, and in the battle between moral values and hierarchical structures- both can win but very few can convey a point that wins its opposers over. Love over agendas is an ideal. Love over agendas is ideal. It is my right to say, there are those that feed on the agitation of others like a leech. Filling up to the point of nausea. The fad diets, the billboard top hits, the conflicting kinesiologists mis-, dis-, and true information, your content is killing you Slowly. Unless, I can heal you now.

"Sure"

Sure.

Are you sure?

Surely you must be mistaken.

Don't be so sure.

Rest assured.

You can never be too sure these days.

Surrreeee.

"S(hhhhh)urre"

I never felt so sure.

Well they sounded sure.

Shoe

Shore

Shhh

Ore

Shurr

Shure?

Sore

Sour

Sun

Shower

Unsure

"Ny"

Ny didn't die, it was I...

When I returned to life I saw vibrance return to the pavement, heard a harmony of sirens and felt the heavy handed tap of sunlight on my exposed shoulders. You've been gone a while. Ny, you noticed me. Now I got you all figured out. You fain pretension because it is you who would like attention. Digital advertising, urgent care, malls and smoke shops are all a local's eye could see beside the exquisitely priced food that we take for granted and the performers begging to be seen. Everything worth it comes at a cost.

You remind me daily.

You and I threatened to break up many times but yet I still hold you tightly not wanting to let go. My eyes fixated on the pedestal that I'm always on the precious of your approval. You wonder where I'm going? Why have I been away so long? Why we don't go out like we used to? We've matured. I know you're seeing other people. I've made my peace with that. But now silence is required when I make my decisions. I contemplated many moments where we could live happily ever after. Embrace me, our story isn't over yet. Erase me, go on and get another pet. Then face, as I submerge through the tunnels. I see the world in a bubble and feel the wonder that you provide.

Ny...Ny. 

A sea of blue and orange spills out into the navy white ocean. Blurs of green with an assortment of red and blue obstruct your path, a shadow is cast by the dark knights of Brooklyn.

"Nola. Pt. 2- The Other Side"

Nola, I love you.
I now stand on the other side of what you made me.
What you took and what you gave me.
I know you know I wasn't crazy.
I was special.
I went from off the rails,
Back to [Grand] Central Station,
To reach my potential.
I love the person who came back.
A brave new soul with his spirit intact.

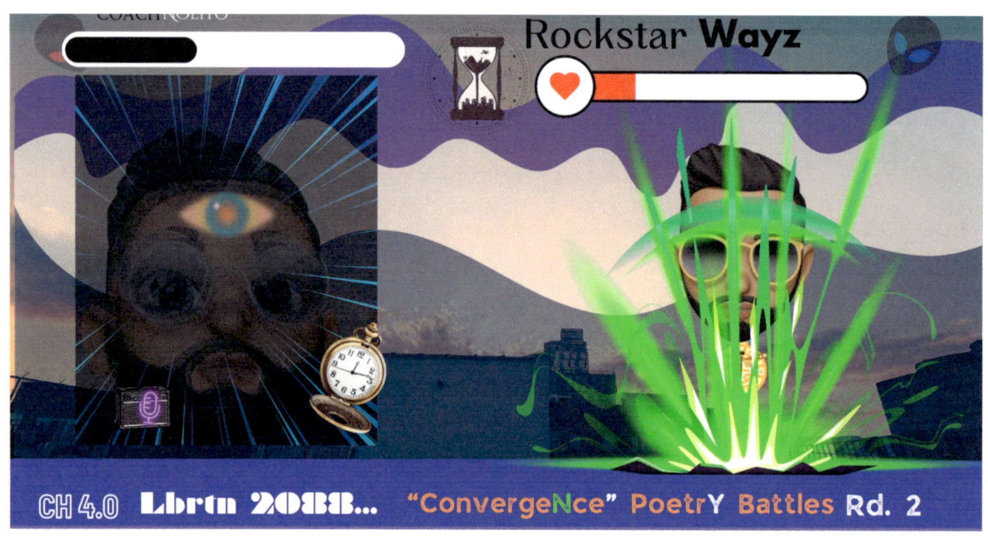

Dear Leon,

Leon, I have written many things. But I've never written to you, my son. I know you were special. Although mom and I never got it figured out, you were our bundle of joy that helped us both to grow up. We were young prideful summer babies who were both concerned about personal commitment until we had to face the reality that you were scheduled to enter our world as both of our collective birthday gifts in early August. I had a lot to learn within the span of 9 months. I would find myself having to tap into parts of myself that I never knew existed and bring about a love that I have never seen nor shown, not even to your mother. A million things crossed my mind as my brain stood blank knowing that much was going to be gained after losing the quantity of possibilities that were previously presented to me. Possibly for the first time in your mothers and in my life, it was not about us. It should have been all about you. But instead, it was about our families, their opinions of us and where it occurred to your mom in that moment that I may not be the right pairing for her. On top of that, at the time, a life of hospitality didn't speak "financially stable". But up until this point I have been able to make ends meet and stand up on my own two feet, individually. Maybe I wasn't ready for a partnership but intrinsically I knew I was ready to sacrifice for you. And I also truly knew I wasn't ready to sacrifice you, but in these types of decisions I am secondary to the one who has to carry you. No, I didn't yet have the money to get married, true. And yes, the road ahead was going to be bumpy too. So now I'm in my mid-thirties, worried that I may no longer be worthy of love and commitment. Up until the point I had to confront the truth that I was still a youth and although I have been aloof, I would still have been your loving father through and through. My little genius capable of accomplishing anything his little heart desired could change a whole room with his micro expressions. The mind of a scientist, the heart of a teacher and the soul of a leader, the life that gives life to art in all of its forms. I only wish I could have looked into your beautiful brown eyes, felt your heartbeat on my fingertips and carried you in my arms as I kissed your cheeks and watched you smile. We never recovered after she aborted you. Yeah, we stood together. No, she barely wanted to touch me. By January we were two people who occupied the same space but our time wasn't quality. My potential, capped by her expectations of me as I was the hurdle standing in the way of her happiness. And I should have told her then what I am telling you now. You would have been the source of mine. To this day I still think of you. I love you more each day and you have instilled in me the ability for forgiveness. Twelve long years have passed. At 24 years of age that was the amount of hours that I spent not taking my life seriously. The last thing I told your mom when she left me that one New Year's, a four year relationship turned to toilet water down the drain, I told her I would change for her. I lied. I never factored her in another decision again. I changed for you. Because in her absence, you looked after me every step of the way. You sent me numerous signs and sent me blessings, literally from the sky above. Now, I'm all grown up. I don't speak to your mom. There is nothing to say to her except "thank you for my child" as he in fact let her give birth to achieving her hopes and dreams as you raised me up to achieve mine.

Love always,
Dad

"Fearless"

What does it take to be fearless? Fearlessness is freedom. So do we choose not to be free? Out of fear comes infidelity, violence, regret. But it also provides safety, love, respect.

The fearless are detached. Willing to cross any line, push any boundary
Scary thought, right? Not to a fearless person.

Let's go back to freedom.

Freedom is a choice. The power to choose how to proceed with life, Independent of someone, anyone's feelings. One could be fearless and still make honest human and decent choices, right?

I'd argue... Ab-soul-utely.

Did someone say soul? For those who believe in the rational soul- the philosophers, theologians, the spiritual and the secular. It's one thing you never share. No one has what I own.

But, you can have this.

"Baby Blue Wayfarers"

These baby blue wayfarers that my sister picked out for me, help me to see the world vividly. Even in the absence of color, these shades change the hue of my environment. As the brightness intensifies, the optics of these lenses maintain warmth. The saturation within these frames drip with a technicolor contemporary motif. These aren't rose colored glasses, these are the baby blue wayfarers that my sister picked out for me.

You can't compare and contrast the two. Because in contrast these so-called sunglasses see things as they actually are. Breath...taking. Choose the setting: Sun, sky, clouds, trees, all phases of the moon, walls, floors, stairs, doors, pillars, posts, mountains, coves, ball games, operas, concerts, retreats. If there's a glimmer of light in your sight and in your spirit, get your sibling to pick out your next set of glasses and tell me what you see.

"Golden Boy" -Chorus

"I had to give up Midas in order to the Golden Boy

I'm announcing my return, so I'll make a song that you won't enjoy.

I had to give up Midas in order to be the Golden Boy.

I'm announcing my return, so I'll make a song that you won't enjoy."

Verse 2- *(The Darkest Parts of Ourselves)*

Detached til' I'm unrecognizable
Pushing out pain, I could handle
But oy, it was sizable
I don't need lovers ; I don't need friends
All of that stuff is now becoming distractions.
I don't need limits, I just need wins
Save your advice for somebody who's asking
And now I'm basking, in the freedom of getting over you
I don't need this job either,
What that chorus do?

'Consensus'

You, the name that has my attention every time. Who has an instant impact on the way that I flow, wherever I go, I've been sour as limes. Cause' I couldn't have ya. And I put it past ya that I was a 6 to ur 9. You know why you've been playing hide and seek all in my mind?

Because I romanticized ya.

And yeah that was me to a fault and although I did halt, I pivoted in many directions since after. Some of the best people you know. I still love them all so. But I know there were still skills left to master. Now, nowhere near close, yes I'm well on my way, despite what they say, I don't need to get there much faster. What needs to be known, now that I'm grown, you have affected every woman thereafter.

Gross.

No, not your fault, not blaming you. But it occurred to me as it might have occurred to you, that you might have had this feeling too... for somebody else.

So, for all the mature women who got over their exes, so I could be at the thread of the nexus, so I can finally address this- that the longest love I ever felt was sexless, when I should have known to love myself. But now when I hear your name. The reaction is still the same, though the name belongs to someone new, my not so subconscious is restless.

My stock has risen, cool.

Now we both meet as 8's, I'm doing quite great, I make sure not to overfill my plate... At any rate, time is not sick, it doesn't have wings but hot damn it flew. Remembering when I was in the palm of your hand, you had the ball tossing me around, but now understand, now that's all through. This is my extraction, I'm removing my attraction, you've become such a distraction. As I have searched for the one who can fill your shoes. I'll rewind 20+ years, to reverse engineer the person who I once considered my muse.

Now I can finally say, I love me too.

The Next Set: Chapter 5 & Beyond

Chapter 5.0 The FoBiA Files: Finding Joy(,)Confronting Fear- Available on Video Download on jayrmidas.com. Video streaming link included with paid Substack subscription. Complimentary Ch. 5- Still Frame Edition Available on Spotify and YouTube!

.

Special Acknowledgements:

The Blessing of Family:
Mom, Dad, Grandma, Grandpa- Jesus (RIP). My Sister, Brother, Uncles, Aunts, Cousins, Annabelle, M, Augustine, Yvette and all family who have passed along. Love and honor to the family and ancestors who are not mentioned here.

Educators & Influences:
Dr. M. Rutigliano, J. Boylan, Coach P. Klyap, Coach C. Stanco, Dr. J. McNamara, Dr. G. Shaw, Father Perricone, Dr. I. Maloney, Mi Murphy., B. Schornack, Dion Jones-LCI, David Bryant, Ma Murphy., W. Rose, J. Rizzo, L. Berman, M. Allen, and a plethora of other influential passings.

Love and respect to all my contemporaries and foreparents in Poetry, Oration, Literacy, and the Arts!

Reflection & Gratitude-

There are way too many people to name. Every person who steps into your daily world has an impact on your life. It is impossible to name everyone but whether we shared a single memory or a lifetime alongside each other, thank you for being such a blessing. To all my friends and mentors, thank you for your love and support as I continue to work every day to give my best to the world. Thank you for sharing, challenging and appreciating my curiosities.

Love and respect to the people who I grew up with during my time living in Marcy. Some of the best and hardest memories of my youth happened in a flash. I was blessed with 2 parents who loved and raised me to apply myself, even when there were many times that I personally didn't want to. My mom is a sweet woman who was not shy about delivering tough love whether the occasion called for it or not. It was through her belief in me and her innate ability to hold her family down that I am anything in this world, and it's time she gets the recognition and peace that she deserves in THIS lifetime. My father, a physically strong and intimidating man with the heart of a child. He is a playful loving man towards his children and I am blessed to have a father who reminds me how proud he is of me early and often. I get a lot of my traits from my parents, though I also get a ton of character from my grandma, my uncles, cousins and my sister. We are a small tight-knit unit who laughs a lot together as we support each other through the various stages of life. My younger brother is a sweet, physically fit and stoic young man who is constantly achieving new pinnacles of training only to be outshined by his humility. My aforementioned grown little sister is my confidante and a true role model. Not only am I proud of my little sister, I look up to her.

Family extends beyond blood when you grow up in and around the streets of what they now call East Williamsburg, Brooklyn. Shout out to my friends from back in the day around the way, many of whom have since moved away from the neighborhood- including me. I'll take this time to show love to David S., Kiel, Kevin, Denise, Miguel, Amanda, Jose E., Jose M., Jorge C., Johnathan V., Sergio, and others who looked after me in school and around the neighborhood. Wherever each of you are in life, may you and your families continue receiving blessings and achievements. Thank you all. David, to this day we are brothers and that is one of the greatest blessings of my life.

The Ring Side Federation era in McCarren Park was filled mostly with joy through the ebbs and flows of time. Friends old and new would begin to make use of this spacious park, which would later be taken over by recreational leagues and summer camps. We who shared this era know that this time was special. Shout out to the All-Stars of the RSF: Anthony (Scythe), Joshua (Pyro), Kiel (CK), David (Shocka), Rondell as himself, Jose (High Voltage), Eddie (Hell's Guardian), Eric (Mimic), Angel and the Garcia brothers and the red hot Extreme Park Wrestling (EPW) crew right from Ridgewood, NY. As for me, I had a whole *"3 Faces"* thing going on. Twister, Fire Angel & Ghetto/Gangsta Zorro. My family is no stranger to the wrestling ring. I credit my older cousin "Dangerous" Dan Payne for his training and lending his knowledge to me. He was trained by his father, the late great Pete McKay of NYC (RIP); who also influenced my uncle Ruben. To Scythe, the true urban legend. We spent many hours planning and producing our weekly show, building out the move lists, telling the stories, the website, the recording, the announcing and OH! The matches. It was a blessing to share our in ring chemistry- I still remember that one moment that we stopped time mid-move. To everyone in the RSF may you all be honored.

Too many people to name in high school (sorry only a short list this time)- Carl, Carmelo, Eugene, Tobias, Jose Ca., Ozzy, Sidney, Annie, Sandy, Kimberly, the legendary Cruz and Jorge Santi, all of my Wrestling teammates and old friends. High School was dope thanks to all of you. Shout out to y'all for carving out a slice of success for yourselves and look forward to sharing more milestones along this long and winding road of time. Carl and Jose- brotherhood built on the mat- I know you both have great strength to overcome the obstacles of life. Carmelo, Eugene and Tobias- from the Handball Court, to the dancefloor, to the big life milestones- life rewards good people, and y'all are top tier.

To my college and my brotherhood, the Beta Sigma Chapter of a well-known national Italian-American heritage fraternal organization. You have placed some of the best people in my path. I have grown and changed so much over the years, citing my professional and personal experience through the time as I shared with a vast array of personalities and beliefs. There are many names I can tout out with glowing reverence such as Pedro, Mark, Jamaal, Pat M, Pat F., Pat R.W., Mike A., Mike C., Eric, Pete, Paul, Eugene, Ray (RIP), James, Chris F. (RIP)., Chris S., Chris T., Danny, Andrew D., Andrew F., Todd, Bryan, Ryan, Kevin F., Kevin M., Kevin N., Jalon, Shareef, Rodney, Paolo only starts the list. It would be remiss if I didn't include my "big brother", Rob. Robby, you were the iron that kept me sharp and have always supported and believed. For that and much more, my appreciation for you knows no bounds brother. You definitely get proof-reading credits on this work; sincerest thank you for your feedback. Look forward to our next project together- Pidgeblack and the Firebreathing Dragonfly!

Suzanne. It feels at times that we have walked around the world and back. The crazy part is it feels like we do it within 30 minutes because time always jumps when we are hanging together. I'm super proud of you and all you have accomplished as a person, as a professional and as a loving mother to your children. May you continue to achieve the goals that you set for yourself as your presence in this world is a gift. Near or far, love you always!

My seven years in restaurant hospitality allowed me to meet some incredible people along the way. People at different stages of their career and their lives shared moments which helped pass the time, especially in our more challenging moments. Blessings to big bro Will, Justin, Salvador *(RIP)*, Jessica, Justin, Darryl, David, Brice, Ebony, Minervah, Shaneeka, Cathy, Kevin, Alexis, Jontel, Jason (Indy), Jonay, Sam, Jari, Bill, Eric, Adam, Eric, Omar, Stephanie, Melyssa, and the list goes on. To all the members of Real Artist Group Entertainment, y'all are the real ones, thank you for taking the first steps of a long journey with me. To William- Big bro, you have made an indelible impact on me. Professionally, you watched me grow up and supported me throughout the years. What you may not hear as often is how much of a great man and role model you are. Your wonderful son knows that better than anybody. Kev, a man who is both debonair and kind hearted who I had the privilege of seeing grow up in real time. Thanks for the laughs and the bonds of true friendship that only someone like you can provide. Stay blessed my brother!

I jumped right into direct work with the youth as a sports coach and physical educator. I have been blessed to encounter some of the best people who do this work. The names are countless. Ben, Kat, Michael, Chondite, Kameica, Crystal, Brandon, Jason, Kazim, Wilson, Sheryl, Enid and Diamond only scratch the surface of the people who I have been fortunate enough to be influenced by over the years. Kat, from supervisor to super-homie, thank you for always seeing the value in me and being a great friend all these years. Kat & Joe, thank you both for your cameo in Chapter 3.5 Ep. 9. Diamond, I appreciate you for joining me on this path and agreeing to deliberate with me when I need a second opinion. You have been an advocate for making sure

I achieve fairness in the professional arena. I wish that for you too. Your belief in me provides strength and assurance that my dreams are worth accomplishing too. May you receive from the world everything you are looking for and more. Chondite- thank you for lending your knowledge to myself and the many others who walked through the doors in the youth coaching space. Your experience and natural instincts with kids, has impacted so many of us positively and I would like to acknowledge that, and you for your presence over the years. Kam, I've grown knowing you- possibly in a way I wouldn't have otherwise. You, surely among others, encouraged my artistic side. My one takeaway in our conversations was that there can be a healthy uniqueness to our personal thinking that others don't have to share. It's a beautiful gift humanity has bestowed upon us. That was something that you imparted on me.

Inversely, while coming up I had to work two part time jobs. My service in Non-Profit after school programming came with many incredible responsibilities and stories. Although during this time corporate benefits didn't come with the work, I received many perks beyond compensation. David D., Darius, Denzel, Stella, Jasmine, Brittany, Natalia, Nahima, Ana, DuQuan (Chris), Taskin, Ralph, Eli O., and Rua are some of the immediate names that instantly come to mind when it comes to developing my personal and professional growth. I have been fortunate to work alongside each of you. I hope that our time together added value and purpose to your lives as well. David, Nahima, Rua and Darius- Thank you all for your trust in me and giving me the platform to lead and influence others.

At some point we meet our metric for growing up. To the founding team of educators and faculty at our second home in the Upper West Side- "This is going to be the hardest job you ever had, you still want it?" was the initial question that was presented to me as this idea came together. Since then, it has opened doors to opportunities that require leadership, poise, care and discernment. From our initial year the family grew to include many contributors to our work environment. Becky, Stephen, Sarah, Wes, Jose, Victor, Jane-Marie, Margot, Pham, Kimm, Shannon, Megan, Paul, Elijah, Jenn, Fredrike, Kenny, Amelia, Jason, Shamair, Monica and a plethora of other amazing professionals represent a fraction of the people I had the privilege to work alongside- thank you for the growth, validation, companionship, motivation and being a pivotal reason to keep getting up each morning and create magic in and beyond the classroom. Becky & Stephen, I reflect back on our time and youthful energy to see clearly the purpose of why we were placed in each other's lives. It has been a blessing to have shared laughs, challenges and perspectives that helped each of us to tap into our better selves and turnkey our experiences to serve others. Amelia, you sought me out and remembered me when I needed to remember myself. Your friendship, love and support always reminded me of how strong I am, as we both stand on the solid foundation of our Borinquen culture. No more ancestral padlocks, only generational blessings based on who we choose to be in this world- genuine, forthright, loving humans who see the world in others.

To Jesse, Larry and Mark- It has been an honor to have learned from you. I gained much under your respective leadership. You put together a fantastic team. Top 4% of educators in the entire world. I hold that proudly. Thank you for the awesome responsibilities you placed upon my shoulders with the belief that I was strong and capable to handle all that came my way. In reflection, I am happy with the professional I've grown into as a result. Thank you very much.

To my podcast brethren - "Don Doe", "Da' Nonymous" and "Rodi": The 3 Random Guyz (3RG) Podcast and Open the Box [To Think Outside of It] respectively were some of the more enjoyable times of my life. Whether getting a chance to explore our irreverent humor through the medium of podcasting or extrapolating an idea to have a different understanding of something that seemed simple and straightforward inevitably lent itself to spending quality time with some of my closest friends while building some foundational skills in the process. In our time we have done some unique work together and improved significantly as time went along. Our crossover episodes were always something special. Special thanks to all the guests who joined us along the way such as Cykon, the Khalessi who lived, BYQ, Incognita and Hu Dis among others. Who knows, perhaps one day we may reprise this project- these streets need a reason to laugh! Rando's Recommendations: Se. 1 Ep. 3 "Le Oops"; Se. 2 Ep. 14 "The 2020 Debate that Matters"; Se. 2 Ep. 19 "Wonder Woman vs. The Bronx" feat. Incognita; Se. 2 Ep. 20 "When You Wish Upon 3 Stars" 3RL (3 Random Ladyz) Podcast; Se. 3 Ep. 33 "The Most Undissable Celebrity/3RG In Space". All Available on Spotify and Apple Podcasts.

My next professional stop would then take me to the West Village... to a place I could only describe as Wonderland. It was here where many blessings were found through obstacles. It was here where I learned to navigate the political atmosphere while maintaining my genuine character in order to truly grow. Here it became definitive that I march to the beat of my own drum and I wouldn't have it any other way. Thank you to those who have held me down, including but not limited to Sean, Chris, Dan, Oscar, Luis, Felix, Helto, Destiny, Alexus, Bibi, Cebo, Emily, Kristina, Jeanette, Nick, Ana, Rosario, Esther, Rosemary, Raymond, Richard, Lindsay, Brandyn, Dean, Natalie, Natalia, Sarah, Matt, James, Vanessa, Amit, Stan, Rosalie, Judy, Daniel, Tim, Juan, Abel and a litany of others who are the living batteries operating this posh building and keeping it's lights on by sheer virtue of their energy. Y'all will always hold a special place in my heart. Natalia, you have always been an amazing human, your kindness is worth the purest gems- plus more. Thank you for connecting me to such a purposeful opportunity and such a warm and friendly environment. Raymond, thank you for our time coaching together; I appreciate all of your contributions on and off the court. Destiny Helto and Daniel, you've deepened my faith in God and myself through our robust and thought provoking conversations. Blessed to remain connected with you Sean, keep making the world laugh- because we all need it! Thank you for Jen, Leslie, Jessica and Sarah- thank you for your time, effort and investment in me as I wish you and the community well in its continued growth and success.

As of this writing I am currently on a new path that is still being forged. I've been up, I've been down and I've been everywhere in between. Now, I'm looking to feel secure in all aspects of my life- physically, emotionally, mentally, spiritually, financially. There are many people that the divine Creator places in our path. The prophetic, Richie Ree and the incomparable Reyla- You are instrumental in my maturation as a person and as an artist. Whether for a moment or for a life span, we are threaded meticulously into the life that was created for us. Thank you to the crew who have given maximum effort to brighten the UWS community through your work- thank you for carving a space for me in your home! - Tessa, Julio, Yesenia et. al.

I've had a hard time opening up over the years. There have been a strong few that I have been cosmically and emotionally tethered to. Thank you for the love and the memories. Your names are omitted because you know you already have my respect; a life of happiness is what I seek for you. Those who know me know I'm the type of person who doesn't like to let go, until I do. As a result, healthy detachment has become an essential part of my personal preservation. Every interaction is divinely purposeful. Some situations have shown to be the right pairing at the wrong time, the wrong pairing at the right time, two good people who had different goals or simply a strong love that had run its course. Whatever the case is, I wish you all well.

My Ode to You and Many More. I've laid on my bed of art, now it's time to stand on business.

Open the Box [To Think Outside of It]
Cover Art By: Gabrielle Jean-Baptiste

3 Random Guyz (3RG) Podcast
Cover Art By: Diana Serquen

So, what's next?

Behold! **Chapter 6:** *Shut Up and Speak!*- Coming in 2025

Chapter 1.1- The Beginning is a Present: Chapter 1 Reimagined with Visuals and Reflections
Chapter 2.1-The Past Returns: Chapter 2 Remastered with Visuals and Reflections

C.A.L.M.- Coming Soon
This one's gonna be big y'all.

A list of my favorite Poets up to June 30, 2024. Life after July 1st will be answered in Chapter 6:
Darius Nazario
Destiny Torres
Jonathan Rua
Kristina Rodriguez
Langston Hughes
Maya Angelou
Nick Morris
Raymond Wang
Rey from High School
Sekou Sundiata
William Shakespeare
That list has grown tremendously since then.

SailorXGarnet

On Midas Make-up Day, I owe you to of my Amazing friends (last week and this week). So here is one of two!

Poetry is Art. Art is Love. Love doesn't always have to agree with our message but it does allow you to have a space in their home. Thank you all for your love, your art, and making a home for me. For the love of the Art there is more in store:

My Bookshelf... The Ones I Read...and Recommend

***-Personal Favorite**

Alex Haley- The Autobiography of Malcolm X As Told to Alex Haley*
Ashlee Vance- Elon Musk
Don Miguel Ruiz- The Four Agreements**
Esmeralda Santiago- When I Was Puerto Rican*
George Orwell- 1984*
James C. Hunter- The Servant
John C. Maxwell- How Successful People Think; Make Today Count; The 360 Leader
Malcolm Gladwell- The Tipping Point; Outliers; What the Dog Saw; Talking to Strangers**
Mark Sanborn- You Don't Need a Title to Be a Leader*
Marx J. Seifer- Wizard: Life and Times of Nikola Tesla
Michael Lewis- Moneyball*
Neil Degrasse Tyson- Astrophysics for People in a Hurry
Nicky Cruz- Run Baby Run
Paolo Coelho- The Alchemist**
Robin Waterfield- Marcus Aurelius Meditations The Annotated Edition*
Roxanne Dunbar-Ortiz- An Indigenous Peoples' History of the United States*
Sarah Moriarty- North Haven**
Sun Tzu- Art of War
William Shakespeare- Power: Vintage Minis

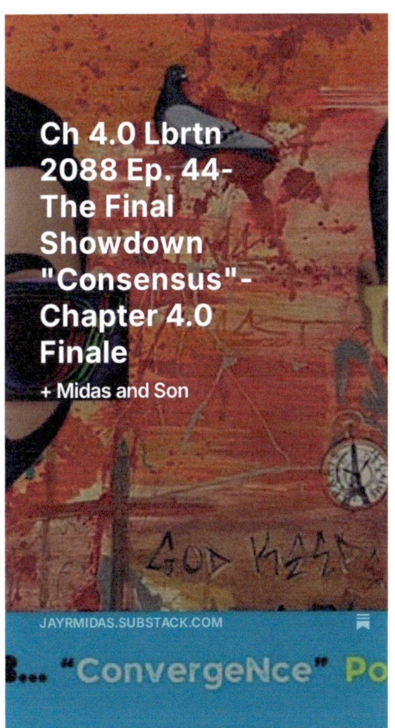

Background Canvas Art:
"American Nightmare"
By Erica Ferman

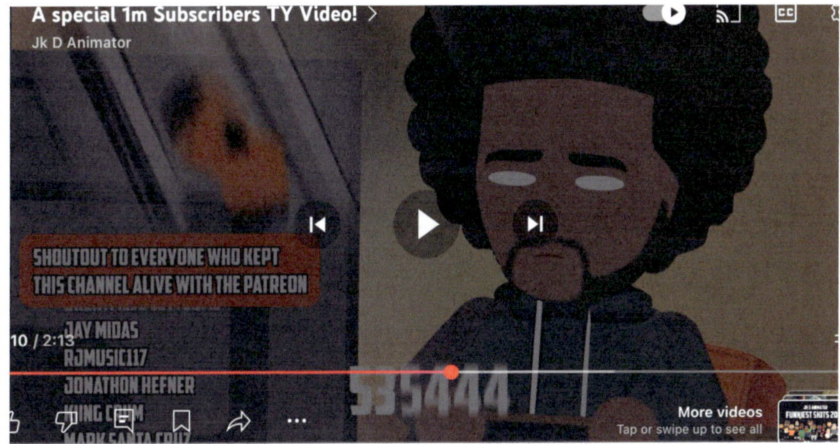

Shout Out to Dragon Flow Z -Reaches 1 Million on YouTube!

This Book Belongs to:

Made in the USA
Columbia, SC
08 January 2025

45d4d6d7-6cce-4f2d-bdd7-a685106cd723R01